BEGINNING
WING
CHUN

Why Wing Chun Works

D1731528

A Peacenik Press Book

Disclaimer
Every effort has been made to ensure that the Chinese terms used in this book have been translated accurately. Should there be any omissions or errors in this respect we apologise and shall be pleased to make corrections where applicable in any future edition.

British Library Cataloguing Publication Data.
A catalogue record for this book is available from the British Library

ISBN 978-0-7552-1457-0

Published in conjunction with
Authors On Line Ltd
19 The Cinques
Gamlingay, Sandy
Bedfordshire SG19 3NU
England

BEGINNING
WING
CHUN

Why Wing Chun Works

Alan Gibson

Acknowledgements

Main photography was by Robert Dunning from Solentstudios. com, David Peterson supplied the Wong Shun Leung photos, Kevin Bell, Kevin McLaren and Christian Riley were models. David Peterson provided the foreword and the 'Loi Lau Hoi Sung, Lat Sau Jik Chung' section, along with much advice, ideas and proofreading. Andre Ibbett helped in the history section; Kevin McLaren wrote the Strength and Conditioning section; Kevin Bell wrote the Fighting Practice section and contributed generally; Mark Page proofread the manuscript. Thanks to all at Summersdale for bringing this book to print, especially Lucy for her patience and understanding during editing. Thanks also to my family – Sarah, Tabitha and Theo – for their continued love and support.

Contents

Foreword

This marks the third time that Alan Gibson has honoured me by inviting me to write an introduction to one of his fine books. In doing so, Alan has effectively taken me full circle with him on his journey along the Wing Chun road. Having offered my limited contributions to his second and third books in this series, I have now been able to actively participate not only in the complete revision and re-writing of the book that started it all, Why Wing Chun Works, but more importantly, to have played at least a small part in Alan's personal discovery of the amazing legacy left to us all by the late and great Wing Chun scientist and philosopher, Sifu Wong Shun Leung.

Having now had six very successful and enjoyable sojourns to the United Kingdom over the past three years, whereby I have been able to interact with Alan and a number of his colleagues in both public and private training sessions, I have witnessed Alan's strong desire to both acquire and share the knowledge and skills associated with the Wong Shun Leung method. His open-minded approach to learning and his passion for teaching comes through strongly in this excellent volume that you now have in your hands.

If you are someone who has read and enjoyed the original work, you will immediately be struck by the detail that has now been added to the text, but at the same time recognise the same reader-friendly style of writing and clarity of presentation that makes Alan's books amongst the best available. If this is the first time that you have read one of Alan's books in the Why Wing Chun Works series, you will soon be rushing out to buy copies of the companion volumes.

Superbly illustrated with hundreds of photos shot especially for this edition, expanded and updated sections on all aspects of the system, and with new detailed sections on training drills and supplementary training concepts, this book is by far the very best available today for anyone seeking a practical approach to personal protection concepts and a better understanding of what the Chinese art of Wing Chun Gung-fu is all about.

With regard to the history, concepts, techniques and most importantly, in terms of appreciating the combat reality of this fighting system as compared with most others practised today, Beginning Wing Chun is one book that no serious martial artist can afford to ignore. Congratulations to Alan on producing this fine book, and congratulations to the reader for choosing to purchase it – you now have the martial arts equivalent of pure gold at your disposal!

David Peterson, Chief Instructor and Founder of Melbourne Chinese
Martial Arts Club

Preface

Wing Chun, also known as Ving Tsun and Wing Tsun, is a system of Chinese kung fu. Originally a secret family system, this sophisticated art was passed on to relatives and close, trusted friends. The effectiveness of Wing Chun as a functional fighting method is well documented; it has been honed over the years to be simple, direct and effective.

Wing Chun employs its unique understanding of bio-mechanics, angles and sensitivity to overcome aggression. The exercises are scientific in approach, and training can be carried out in a friendly atmosphere of co-operation as opposed to one of competition. With regular and correct training, it is possible for a novice to become competent within one year, although, as with any true art, practical ability is only the beginning. There is always room for deeper exploration, further development and personal interpretation.

'Self-defence is only an illusion, a dark cloak beneath which lurks a razor-sharp dagger waiting to be plunged into the first unwary victim. Whoever declares that any weapon manufactured today, whether it be a nuclear missile or a .38 special, is created for self-defence, should look a little more closely in the mirror. He is either a liar or is deceiving himself.

Wing Chun kung fu is a very sophisticated weapon – nothing else. It is a science of combat, the intent of which is the total incapacitation of an opponent. It is straightforward, efficient and deadly. If you're looking to learn self-defence, don't study Wing Chun. It would be better for you to master the art of invisibility.'

Wong Shun Leung (1935–1997)

Introduction

Updating this book to reflect my present practice has been a fascinating and very satisfying process. Some elements remain unchanged but I have replaced large sections and made countless small (but significant) changes to the remaining text. It's not that anything in the previous version was wrong per se, just that my personal training regime changes as my experience grows. Wing Chun is a journey not a destination. I have worked hard on improving my writing skills to produce a new edition which is more concise and contains a wealth of new information, including a detailed section on drills and supplementary training methods.

It is important to realise that in Wing Chun we are taught concepts, with which we aim to improve our fighting skills. Wing Chun is not about predetermined moves but about feeling; both on an emotional and physical level. So, when someone asks you, 'What would you do if I did...?', your answer should be something like: 'I have no idea, why don't you try to attack me and we'll see what I feel like doing.'

The Chinese names for moves used in this book are the versions and spellings preferred by Sigung Wong Shun Leung. They have been translated by David Peterson, and a full glossary is included in the back pages. It will enhance your perception of Wing Chun if you understand that the names of the various moves are generally verbs as opposed to nouns. In other words, they are describing actions and not positions.

The drills in this book have been set out roughly in the order that they might be taught to a beginner, although it is good practice, not to mention refreshing, to vary the routine of your training. It should be easy to see that simple ideas later expand into more complex movement theories. It is simple to break down any of the basic building blocks of the system, in order to test them and to better your understanding of their functional application.

Some of the training elements, such as strength and conditioning and general fence work, should be integral at all levels of training. Indeed, even the most basic of drills need to be constantly reiterated – no matter how skilled you believe yourself to be. A Chinese saying springs to mind: 'Yet Daam, Yi Lik, Saam Gung Fu,' literally translated as 'First courage, second power, third talk about your skill.' You need courage to fight in the first place; then enough power to hurt your opponent when you attack him. Once you have these qualities, then (and only then) is it meaningful to talk about your skill.

It is a good habit to consider where the element that you are training comes from in the forms. If you always cross-reference your learning, it will give solo practice greater meaning. It also means that you will be doing mental training as you perform your forms on a daily basis. Once you begin to see the similarities between the forms and how they expand ideas, you will also see connections with other elements of fighting and become able to think in a Wing Chun way. However, always bear in mind the very wise words of Sigung Wong Shun Leung and remember to keep things simple, direct, efficient and above all effective.

What Makes A Good Coach?

I prefer the term coach, as opposed to instructor, sifu etc., because it implies that it is possible to improve the skill of a person who is a better fighter than you are. This becomes more significant as you grow older. I will never be the best fighter in the world but I aim to be the best teacher that I can. Teaching on any level requires good communication skills and an open mind. Students should be encouraged to enquire (verbally and physically) about what they are learning. You should never do something just because you have been told to or because it's traditional. In the same way you should never be refused information because 'It's a secret'.

If a student asks a question it should be answered in a clear, precise manner, taking into account the level of understanding of the student. It should not be hidden away under a thick veneer of mystical language and mumbo jumbo. This kind of attitude is at its best unhelpful and at its worst, deceptive. Many martial arts are shrouded in mystery and controversy; this is in no way beneficial to anybody wishing to learn. There are no secrets in Wing Chun, only different interpretations, other ways of expressing your skill.

A coach should be respected for their ability to teach well. You should never fear your teacher; intimidation is a tactic used by the insecure to disguise their own inadequacies. In the end what matters to a student is not the race of the coach, not how strong or fast, nor even how skilful or highly certified the coach is, but how well they can communicate skill.

Once a student has learned a skill it is a good idea for them to explain the theory to, or practise it with beginners. This will not only consolidate their understanding but will also help to groom them to be good coaches themselves in the future.

Why Some Wing Chun Is Different

As with any art we learn our skill from a coach and then, as we progress, a personal style will begin to develop. Eventually our style will be quite different to that of our teachers. This is because we have the ability to think for ourselves, we are not robots. Innovation is normal, healthy and in the nature of all arts; life would be incredibly dull if there was no variety.

As long as we stay within the ideas set down for the style there are no restrictions. Wong Shun Leung was very fond of saying, 'Do not be a slave to the system.' It's OK to have a difference of opinion and fighting is often a good way to settle technical arguments.

Cross training will make you a more rounded martial artist and can only be beneficial to all concerned. Through this process a student can learn to deal with a wider spectrum of situations and become accustomed to the diverse ways in which different styles use technique and energy. Of course some people will never concede to another person's point of view, but one is not always right and the other wrong: sometimes both are correct in different ways, or on different levels of understanding.

Tradition, History and Legend

Much of the ancient history of Wing Chun is legend, deeply embellished for political reasons, and as such, cannot be proven. There are many different versions of its past. Much of the documentation that may have existed has been destroyed, either in the burning of the Shaolin temple, or during the Cultural Revolution. As a result of this, 'evidence' often tends to be constructed out of hearsay and cannot always be considered reliable. The movements of Yip Man during his life are well documented by his eldest son Yip Chun in the book Grandmaster Yip Man Centenary Birth (1993).

The Shaolin Temple

The Shaolin temples are known to have been important in the teaching of kung fu, as well as the development of secret societies such as the Triads, White Lotus, Eight Trigrams, and the Boxers. The first Shaolin temple was situated in Henan province, built around AD. 495 by Emperor Xiao Wen of the Northern Wei dynasty.

Shaolin was very influential in spreading Buddhism in the East. The main temple is situated at the foot of the Songshan or 'Central Mountain' in China. The temple was originally built for an Indian monk known to the Chinese as Batuo. His statue can often be found in Chinese Buddhist monasteries a large, friendly monk.

Later in the sixth century AD another Indian monk, Bodhidharma, known as Da Mo in Chinese, visited the Shaolin temple where he taught meditation techniques to the monks. His teachings became the foundation of a new school of Buddhism known as Chan in China and later Zen, in Japan. The monks had to withstand long periods of meditation, so to help them overcome fatigue, Da Mo taught them breathing techniques and exercises that are thought to have been the start of the martial arts.

At its most prosperous time, about 1300 years ago, the temple housed around 1500 monks, 500 of whom were skilled in combat. The Emperor Tai Zong asked the temple to train a small force of fighting monks that he could rely on whenever he was in danger. The grateful emperor tried to persuade these monks to be full time bodyguards at his court, but they turned him down, saying it was also their duty to protect the Shaolin temple and the monks who lived there.

Around 1000 years later another emperor asked the temple for help. In 1674, 128 monks led by a former Ming partisan Zheng Guande, went to the aid of the Qing Emperor Kangxi. Zheng had previously fought against the Manchu Emperors and then retired to the temple to study. The fighting monks were a great help to the Emperor but after the battle they too turned down the chance of working full time for the Emperor, preferring instead to return to the temple.

The Emperor was persuaded that it was an insult to be turned down in this manner, so he sent an army led by a renegade monk, Ma Ningyi, to attack the monastery. Only a few monks survived the attack and the temple was burned to the ground. According to folklore, five of the surviving monks set out to devise new and better fighting systems.

They became known as the Five Ancestors, or The Venerable Five, and are believed to be responsible for the surviving Shaolin styles. As their original arts took many years to master, it was deemed critical that any new art could be taught in a far shorter time, as existing masters were surrendering to the Manchu government.

Mid 1600s

The monks started to develop the principles of this new art but before it could be put into practice the temple was raided again with the loss of many monks. One of the escapees was a Buddhist nun named Ng Mui. She was the eldest and most proficient in boxing skills. With her acquired knowledge and with the aid of some documentation written by the murdered monks, she taught a young girl with the name Yim Wing Chun (Beautiful Springtime), representing hope for the future. The system was later named after her and she is said to have used it to successfully repel an unwanted suitor.

1700–1800

In time, Yim Wing Chun married and shared her knowledge with her husband Leung Bok Cho who became a very proficient exponent of the art. Leung Bok Cho passed his skills on to a herbalist called Leung Lan Kwai who in turn taught Wong Wah Bo who worked with an opera troupe called the Red Junk. Legends abound about the Red Junk and it was there that Leung Yee Tai was introduced to the art. He was the pole man for the Red Junk and had been shown how to use the boat's pole for fighting by one of the temple elders, reputedly venerable monk Jee Shin.

So the pole form was introduced to the system. The butterfly knives were, possibly, also introduced around the time of the Red Junk.

End of 1800s

This is where more reliable documentation begins.

Around 100 years ago Leung Jan, a skilled physician in Foshan, was one of the chosen few to receive training in Wing Chun.

He was greatly respected by his community as a gentleman who never boasted about his kung fu. Next door to Leung Jan lived a moneychanger by the name of Chan Wa Sun. He was a powerful fighter who also respected his neighbour for his skills. Chan Wa Sun asked Leung Jan to teach him.

Eventually Leung Jan decided to teach Chan Wa Sun, but being a large and strong man he did not teach him in the same way that he taught his sons Leung Bik and Leung Chun, who were of smaller build and therefore needed different skills to overcome stronger opponents. Later, Leung Bik travelled to Hong Kong and Chan Wa Sun remained in Foshan where he built up a following.

1899–1905

Amongst his students was a young boy named Yip Man. Yip Man offered Chan Wa Sun 300 silver pieces in return for tuition. At first Chan Wa Sun refused thinking the money stolen, but after a visit to the boy's parents he discovered that he had worked hard to earn the money and, being suitably impressed he took him on as a student.

Yip Man studied for four years under the instruction of Chan Wa Sun and after his death, following his master's wishes, he continued to train under Ng Chung So in order to complete the system.

1908

Yip Man travelled to Hong Kong to study at college. By now the young Yip Man had quite a reputation as a fighter. Through some friends he was introduced to an eccentric old scholar renowned for his skills. The old man was no other than Leung Bik, the surviving son of Leung Jan, who had been taught a more subtle technique by his father. Leung Bik accepted Yip Man as a student and taught him many new diverse methods. In time Yip Man returned to Foshan with his new knowledge. For the next 20 years he worked for the army and the police, he also married and had four children. The Japanese invasion of Southern China came in 1937. During these hard times he continued his training and in 1941 started to teach the first generation of students.

1948

After the war, in 1948, the communist government took over. Yip Man had to leave everything behind and go to Macau.

Eventually he returned to Hong Kong with Leung Sheung, who was to become his first Hong Kong student, and set up a Wing Chun school at the Restaurant Workers Union building, where his reputation, as both a skilful fighter and teacher of Wing Chun began to grow.

Yip Man's moves to Macau and then Hong Kong were very significant for the development of Wing Chun; had he remained in China, the art as it was traditionally taught may have been changed. The communists regarded martial arts as defiant and outdated. They altered the content of many, adding new theatrical and acrobatic moves to enhance their appeal renaming them Modern Wushu. The communist government infused these new arts with western competitive sporting ideals, and promoted modern Wushu, both as a means of strengthening the spirit of the socialist state, and also as a method of bringing to an end the secretive, rebellious aura that had surrounded martial arts in the past.

Over the next 22 years Yip Man taught many students, several of whom have gone on to become masters in their own right and spread the skills of Wing Chun throughout the entire world. Yip Man died at his home in Hong Kong on the 1st December 1972 at the age of 79. His sons Yip Chun and Yip Ching continue to teach Wing Chun.

During this period the Yip Man taught his system to a fighter named Wong Shun Leung. Wong in turn developed his own interpretation of the style based around his experience of Beimo or challenge fighting. He was a peerless and intelligent pugilist. Throughout his many Hong Kong challenge fights, in which he fought champions from many different martial arts styles, he remained indomitable. Wong named his style Ving Tsun Keun Hok (Scientific Wing Chun – he preferred the VT spelling as opponents of the style had taken to referring to it as 'toilet fist' because of the English style of using WC as an abbreviation of lavatory). It was forged in the fire of battle to be simple, direct and efficient. Wong was also well known as Bruce Lee's mentor and coach (although Lee was technically a student of Yip Man) and continued to exchange ideas with him up until Lee's death. Wong Shun Leung passed away on 26 January 1997. His students continue to teach Wing Chun all over the world.

1970s

Bruce Lee was of course, the most famous of Yip Man's students. Lee was already well known in the East as an actor in the Hong Kong film industry. With the Hollywood blockbuster Enter The Dragon he shot to fame across the world. With the success of this film in the seventies there was an explosion of interest in kung fu and oriental culture in the West.

Wing Chun still enjoys its rich heritage and history, and thanks to the endeavours and curiosity of the great number of practitioners today, it is still living, expanding and moving forward as an art, a skill, and as a very practical way of fighting.

Pic. 1

Wong Shun Leung

Pic. 2

Wong Shun Leung, with his student David Peterson

Wing Chun Principles

Triangulation

Wing Chun's strength comes from its structure or skeletal architecture; this is more simply explained by looking at the body in terms of shape. Triangles or pyramid shapes are both strong, and easy to understand.

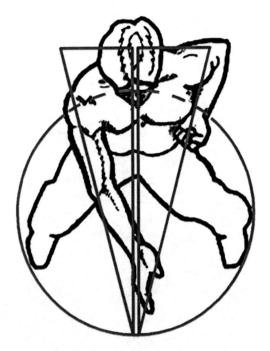

Pic. 3

Looking at the body in terms of shape will make the Wing Chun principles easier to understand and enhance learning

Triangulation is easy to understand and apply because of the way our bodies are jointed. The stance is strong and stable because of its triangulation; this supports the upper body, which gives a firm board for the triangulated arm actions to work from. We need to make our hand/arm shapes act like a wedge. This will cause our enemy and their attacks to be deflected (Pic 3).

We can then think about driving this wedge into the centre or down our opponent's guard. When employed correctly, triangulation will enable our limbs to contain the strength of angles, as opposed to the over-use of muscular strength. This is superior because it allows the limbs to remain relaxed, enabling them to move quickly and freely, unhindered by muscular tension.

Some styles of Wing Chun tend to use a longer triangle with the apex (point of contact) at the wrist, whereas others, notably Wong Shun Leung's Ving Tsun, tend to work at a closer range, using the elbow to control the enemy and leaving the hand free to hit.

Pic. 4

Central Axis Theory

The pivot is made easier to understand by application of central axis theory. This concept is, on its simplest level, an imaginary line or plane that extends outward from your centre – normally towards your enemy. It could be described as the direction of your attention or intent. Significantly, it is also the shortest path between your body and that of your enemy.

When out of contact, Mun Sau (Inquisitive Hand) and Wu Sau (Rear/Guarding Hand) will normally both lie on the centre line (Pic. 5a and b). This line is used to help detect, or interpret the direction of incoming forces in order to feel which action is appropriate. When the central axis line is occupied correctly, the opponent is forced to attack down a longer path than that taken by your own attack. In this situation the only other alternative for an opponent is to attempt to force the central axis line using strength.

If force is used to counter an attack it can quickly be capitalised upon. From a strong position, an attack can be launched which cannot be stopped without the use of strength. If we make use of the Wing Chun concepts and attack with simple and direct strikes, we are more likely to be successful. Opponents who become frustrated over-commit their attacks, and will feed us with the information we require to defeat them. Of course in fighting, other elements, such as physical and mental conditioning and courage, will all come into play.

Pic. 5a   Pic. 5b

The central axis line is an imaginary plain that moves with us. It helps to simplify, or aim our triangulation

Clearly it is desirable to occupy the central axis line effectively. It is also essential to attack on centre; this is not always the same as the central axis line and not just because vulnerable points lie down the centre of the body.

When we strike our opponent we want the blow to have maximum effect upon them. We want all the force generated in our attack to go into them. If we want the opponent to absorb all the weight of the strike, they must not be allowed to pivot in order to return or dissipate its energy. This is the reason for attacking the centre.

If the blow lands centrally the enemy soaks up all the energy and is propelled backwards or driven off their stance. They are consequently unable to lose any force by pivoting and only able to generate ineffectual counter attacks. It is important to note at this point, that the centre is a line drawn from the source of the incoming force to the core (or central axis) of the body. This is not the same as a line drawn along the front of a body unless the attack is coming in straight and, square on the body (See Pic. 6).

The Wing Chun straight-line punch will normally land square on if it comes from the inside line. However, if it comes in from outside the arm of the opponent it must hit the body at an angle, allowing for the width of the attacker's shoulders, and the direction of the line into the core. We must make sure that our energy acts through our opponent's central axis (although it is perfectly possible to knock someone out by clipping them). An example of this would be if a snooker or pool player wishes the cue ball to stop dead, after striking a coloured ball. The shot would have to be played square. If the coloured ball was struck at an angle the cue ball would continue to move after impact, so it has not imparted all its energy to the other ball.

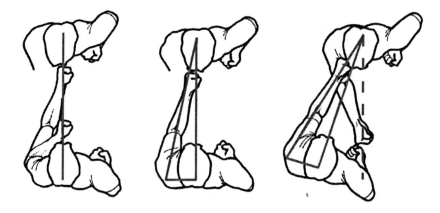

Pic. 6

Strikes should be aimed at the centre of the body making it more difficult for the opponent to pivot. This allows the strike to have maximum effect

Pic. 7

Combining these principles we can see that: as you pivot (or step) out of the path of an incoming attack, the counter is made back into the centre but down a new angle. Triangulation helps to deflect the attack whilst maintaining a strong position

Contact Reflexes

Due to the close range, reactionary nature of Wing Chun, responses are quickly programmed into the neural system of the practitioner and become reflexive. This enables the practitioner to react far faster than would be possible with a visual reflex. The correct reflex is instantaneous and needs to be, given the speed at which fights occur.

Contact reflexes also give the mind more time to concentrate on other aspects, like strategy. Without the use of this method, it would be necessary to see and understand the nature of each attack, choose an appropriate defence and then act accordingly. This is not necessary with a contact reflex as the response is immediate.

The exercises and drills of Wing Chun train the arms and hands to act as sensors to enable us to feel the direction, strength and speed of threats. The movements and hand shapes that we use are a result of our opponent's actions. Remember that the movement involved in making the change from one position to the next is more important than the final position.

Our arms and stance must also act as shock absorbers. It is possible that a movement may be too fast for us to react to or so insignificant, that a reaction is not merited. In these cases we need to buffer ourselves, until such a time as we can be clear about what is happening. The ability to achieve these levels of skill is attained by training in the Wing Chun drills.

Loi Lau Hoi Sung, Lat Sau Jik Chung

It pays at this point to remember a famous couplet that illustrates the Wing Chun system in a nutshell. The Loi Lau Hoi Sung, Lat Sau Jik Chung concept of Wing Chun is, in essence, the very basis of how this system actually operates. If you like, it is the perfect summary of how Wing Chun (and in particular, the Wong Shun Leung Method) works. 'Loi Lau' refers to engaging the enemy, literally, 'When it comes, stay with it'. In other words, we must form a bridge with the attack by intercepting the path that it takes. In my experience, this is best achieved by utilising a soft approach, whereby there is little or no rigidity in the arm that first engages, but instead a spongy approach where the skeletal strength is used, supported by relaxed muscular action. This is what we seek to develop every time we practise the first section of Siu Nim Tau (the first form). The Loi Lau aspect of this concept encompasses both Siu Nim Tau and Cham Kiu (the second form) ideas.

'Hoi Sung' makes reference to the importance of taking advantage of the opponent's errors by following his centre of mass whenever he/she withdraws a hand/leg/body. Normally, and in keeping with the basic principles of human motion and physics, whenever one moves one limb forwards, they will normally move another limb or part of the body in an opposite direction to counterbalance their position. Well trained Wing Chun practitioners are not so prone to this 'error' as we learn, particularly through Chi Sau (Sticking-hands Exercise) and related drills, to move our limbs quite independently of each other, whereby quite often one arm may well be attacking while the other arm remains totally still and in control of the opponent's hands. Thus, if and when an enemy tries to withdraw the limb, or indeed the whole body, complying with the Hoi Sung concept implies that we immediately follow that withdrawal and seek a pathway to attack, or at least further control and dominate the situation. What it does not imply is that we chase the hands without thought.

The final part of the couplet, 'Lat Sau Jik Chung' is most definitely the most important part of the rhyme, and the part of it most quoted by Wong Shun Leung as a means of summarising his approach to Wing Chun. In essence, it refers to the springy force of Wing Chun. 'When the hands are released, attack directly without hesitation,' is a very literal translation of this verse (a Chinese colleague of mine, who does not practise martial arts, when shown this verse read it as 'Attack without any worries') which best describes what we are trying to develop firstly through the Siu Nim Tau form (in the first section), and then to further enhance it through Chi Sau and other drills. Wong

Shun Leung often stated that this was the difference between good Wing Chun and excellent Wing Chun, meaning that the practitioner who could utilise the Lat Sau Jik Chung concept was the one who would be victorious most often. Again, this involves relaxation and the use of soft resistance against greater force; this will apply even when the arms are well off the central axis line because the elbow will always find its way back to the centre and drive the fist/palm, etc directly towards the opponent's centre of mass.

To better understand and develop all three attributes, practise Siu Nim Tau form, slow down and relax, check and correct the body structure, and work simple drills with like minded training partners.

Simultaneous Attack and Defence

Simultaneous attack and defence does not only mean doing one thing with one hand (defending), and something different with the other (attacking). In Wing Chun this happens most of the time. Simultaneous attack and defence also refers to one hand serving two purposes at once.

By dominating the central axis line, rather than chasing the hands of an opponent, it is possible to deflect an attack and launch an assault on the opponent's centre at the same time, with only one arm. Frequently the situation arises where the elbow is controlling an arm whilst the hand and wrist are still free to attack the centre.

Using elbow position to control the enemy, as opposed to desperately clinging on with the hands, will help you be powerful and yet relaxed. This is because you engage the larger and far more strong muscle groups in the back and chest as opposed to the smaller, weaker arm muscles.

Pic. 8

More Power to Your Elbow

Wing Chun coaches often talk about elbow energy. This is a method of helping people to understand how to use the correct muscles for maximum power, whilst avoiding tension in the arm.

Elbow positioning is used extensively in Wing Chun to defend by deflection, and to pin, trap or control an opponent's limbs. When attacking, the palm or fist is normally kept upright and high if it is on the inside of a limb (utilising Taan Sau concept). This has the effect of maintaining the elbow's outward leverage. If your limb is on the outside of the opponent's limb, the elbow needs to be kept in and down, to jam the centre (utilising Fook Sau concept); this has the effect of angling the fist or palm slightly off vertical. Note the difference between the Jing Jeung and Waang Jeung palm strikes at the end of the first, and the beginning of the third section of Siu Nim Tau as described in Solo Forms.

Efficient Use of Energy or Force

The aim in Wing Chun is to be as efficient as possible, achieving the best results, with the minimum of effort. To this end it is necessary for the arms to be relaxed when they are in motion: this will enable them to change shape in a fast yet fluid way. Tension is only introduced momentarily, usually on the impact of a strike, or on arrival at a specific position. After a blow is landed the limb is returned to its relaxed state immediately, thus allowing further movement.

Attacking moves must be sent forward in a non-committed and relaxed way; as soon as the attack deviates from the target, or the angle is covered, it must be changed. Do not try to force a line, instead adjust the angle, or modify the shape. The fact that an attack did not get through should indicate that a change is due.

Other advantages of staying relaxed during training include being more likely to use the correct muscles and less likely to suffer from fatigue; this in turn allows you to enjoy training for longer periods of time.

Wing Chun is well known for its speed and ability to generate explosive power from very close range. This skill is largely down to correct structure, using muscles efficiently and whole body movement. If you ask someone to make their arm strong they will normally tense up all the muscles, both biceps and triceps, to make all the muscles bulge out. It looks and feels strong. However, because the two muscle sets work antagonistically, there is no functional strength at all. We should really ask the question: 'Strong in which direction?'

When a weight lifter performs a bench press his biceps will be totally relaxed, allowing the triceps, deltoids and pectorals to have maximum effect. It follows that the Wing Chun punch does not use the biceps, except to stop the arm extending too far and to make minute adjustments. Any opposing tension in the upper arm would slow down the dynamic action of the punch.

The position of the elbow, in alignment with the shoulder, wrist and knuckles and the application of tension at the moment of impact, helps to achieve a clean transfer of energy into the opponent. Immediately afterwards the arm must return to its relaxed state, to enable further changes. The efficient use of muscles and joint angles should be studied in the forms and used in every action. Essentially, if you remain relaxed you will be faster, stronger and less constrained in your movements. It also allows you to be sensitive to gaps in your enemy's attack, letting them show you how to hit them.

Short Force and the Inch Punch

Wing Chun is renowned for its 'Inch Punch'. This is actually a party trick and whilst it is good fun to demonstrate it on disbelieving friends, the real purpose of short force is to enable the practitioner to hit from an extended position, without initially withdrawing the arm. This idea is shown in the second section of Siu Nim Tau form.

With correct training, it is easy to master short force. If you achieve correct muscle tension, joint alignment and stance movement, you will hit with the weight of your moving body, as opposed to just the weight and acceleration of your limb. Using the stance to help you hit will ensure maximum power with minimum commitment. It is possible to deliver short force from most major joints including, the elbows, shoulders, feet, knees and even the hips.

Importance of Stance and Posture

The Wing Chun stance is frequently misunderstood because, at first glance and when first practised, it seems to be awkward. However, as with many other aspects of the art, once the mechanics and theory have been understood, it starts to make a lot more sense. Understanding the relationship between the ground (or our feet) and our hands, is vital.

Boxers understand the mechanics involved in hitting off the floor, gaining power by rotating the trunk and developing speed by accelerating the shoulder joint forward. Karate practitioners use a twist of the hips to generate power. Wing Chun uses the stance and footwork to develop tremendous speed, accuracy and power without over-committing the body weight (hence compromising balance).

The normal, Wing Chun Yi Ji Kim Yeung Ma (Character Two Goat Gripping Stance) is a training stance and whilst performing Siu Nim Tau you are actually training both of your rear legs, in readiness for the forward stance and kicking.

The weight should be balanced roughly equally between the legs, allowing for strong easy movement. The rear leg is our connection with the ground, allowing us to press forwards or upwards, to accelerate and to absorb incoming forces or pressure. The front leg prevents us from being pulled forward, or our arms from being pulled down. Any stance is only strong in two directions, so it is important to aim it correctly, and to be able to move quickly and naturally from one position to another.

The pelvis must be rotated forwards, and kept level: this allows you to press or hit without committing your weight. The point of balance should be roughly mid-way between the heels. The legs should feel springy and mobile, not stiff and restricted.

When pivoting it is important to keep the weight on the heels (Pic. 9b). This is aided by keeping the head back and the spine straight (look down your nose at your opponent). The knees must be kept in alignment with the feet. This will avoid any sideways stress on the knee joint. It also helps to cover the groin and rear leg when moving forward or backward and will make foot sweeps less effective.

Movement in the upper body must be created from the stance rather than the back or shoulders (as seen in Pic. 12), which will cause you to reach in and lose triangulation. After turning, we are effectively in a forward stance, facing sideways, depending on where the centre line is. The turn also needs to be sensitive to force.

Pic. 9a   Pic. 9b   Pic. 9c

Pic. 9d   Pic. 9e

Keep your weight central and over the heels, do not lean back. If you turn on the toes your body will swing about, making precision movement impossible. Also you will not be able to press the centre without commitment.

The lead leg also acts as brake when we go forward, stopping over-commitment during an advance, and can be used to push off if we need to move backwards or change direction. The strength of any strike, or defence depends to a large extent on the stability of the stance. Without a strong stance we do not have a solid base to hit from.

The power of a strike relies on acceleration, movement of bodyweight, structure and strength. Weight cannot be changed. Speed and strength can be developed, with the correct use and training of the muscles. But technique can be improved dramatically by an understanding of where power comes from in the stance. The ability to utilise our body weight comes from the ground because we push against it with our feet and legs.

Stance Testing

Pic. 10a   Pic. 10b

Stance dynamics. Pushes and pulls can be resisted if the stance is strong in the right direction

In a basic stance, get a partner to push against your Taan Sau (Spreading-hand Deflection) and feel the force being absorbed in your stance (Pic. 10a and b). If the stance starts to collapse, take a small step backwards, to release the pressure, and reassert your stance, sliding the front leg over to cover the groin. Similarly, you can try pushing a punch up and out against pressure from a partner (Pic. 11). This will test the stability and effectiveness of your structure. If the arm is suddenly released, it should spring forward into a punch. The front foot acts as a stop to prevent committed forward motion of the body.

Pic. 11

Push against a punch to test structure

Then get your partner to pull forward on your Taan Sau or on the back of your neck. Do not allow your body to tip forward, or turn. Feel the pressure going into your front leg. Pull back, wedging your feet against the ground as in a tug of war. If the stance starts to tip over, take a small step forward and reassert your front leg, shuffling the rear leg up to adjust the posture.

Pic. 12

Do not allow the stance to be compromised by bending at the waist or reaching in

Pivoting to Recycle Force

When pivoting it is necessary for the body to act like a rotating cylinder. If a pressure is applied to any point on its circumference it will spin in the same direction as the force. Remember though, that if one side of the cylinder rotates back, the other side is driven forward.

When a force is applied to a Wing Chun practitioner's body or arms, they should pivot in order to deflect the attack or attacker (Pic. 13a and b). The counter-attack is launched utilising the movement of bodyweight to add power and deflect the incoming force off your central axis. The pivoting action can also shift the centre out of the path of the attack.

Pic. 13a   Pic. 13b

Pivoting to deflect force away from the central axis line and striking

Simplicity

Another aspect that contributes to the success of Wing Chun is its simplicity: rather than employ a great amount of different techniques, Wing Chun practitioners strive to understand thoroughly the variety of ways in which a few, simple techniques can be adapted to many different situations.

The fundamental positions are given in the first form, Siu Nim Tau (Young Idea), where we understand the actions relative to a stationary partner – directly in front of us. These ideas are then expanded upon and added to, in the second form, Cham Kiu (Seeking or Crossing the Bridge), where pivoting, tracking, stepping and kicking are introduced, along with the simultaneous use of both hands, leading to the understanding of how to track down and fight a mobile enemy.

Drills like Daan Chi Sau (Single Sticking-hands Exercise), Laap Sau (Deflecting-hands Exercise) and Chi Sau then allow us to progressively explore all the possible combinations and varieties of technique, whilst in full motion. This systematic learning process gives practitioners easily understandable targets to aim at. As each level is absorbed it is then integrated and expanded upon.

The Basic Shapes and Footwork Types of Wing Chun

The most frequently occurring actions in Wing Chun are: Bong Sau, Taan Sau, and Fook Sau.

Pic. 14a

Pic. 14b

Pic. 14c

Wing Chun essentially revolves around these three actions, combined with the stance, striking and kicking. It is essential to gain an in-depth understanding of them; this means not only how and when to apply them but also how they can shift from one to another and how stepping or turning can alter the effect they have. A clear understanding of the many different ways in which these shapes can be used will result in proficient and effective Wing Chun. This may seem an over simplification, but to master the subtle aspects of these moves can take a lifetime.

Taan Sau

Taan Sau is derived from the word meaning spreading out or dispersing and this is how the action is used in application. This test however, demonstrates the potential forward strength of Taan Sau when used correctly, in conjunction with good structure. When Fook Sau presses forward, press Taan Sau back towards your partner's shoulder, using your stance and bringing your elbow near to their wrist to disrupt their stance. Your partner can apply a great deal of pressure downwards on Taan Sau and it will remain strong.

Pic. 15a　　　　　　　　Pic. 15b

Fook Sau

Fook Sau is derived from the Chinese word meaning to bow down or prostrate oneself. This effect is exactly what we attempt to achieve on our opponent when we utilise this action against them. Start with square, facing stances. One person uses Taan Sau and presses towards the partner's chest, Taan Sau should be 90 degrees to the body and positioned between the centre line and the outside of the hip. The other

Pivoting to Recycle Force

When pivoting it is necessary for the body to act like a rotating cylinder. If a pressure is applied to any point on its circumference it will spin in the same direction as the force. Remember though, that if one side of the cylinder rotates back, the other side is driven forward.

When a force is applied to a Wing Chun practitioner's body or arms, they should pivot in order to deflect the attack or attacker (Pic. 13a and b). The counter-attack is launched utilising the movement of bodyweight to add power and deflect the incoming force off your central axis. The pivoting action can also shift the centre out of the path of the attack.

Pic. 13a   Pic. 13b

Pivoting to deflect force away from the central axis line and striking

Simplicity

Another aspect that contributes to the success of Wing Chun is its simplicity: rather than employ a great amount of different techniques, Wing Chun practitioners strive to understand thoroughly the variety of ways in which a few, simple techniques can be adapted to many different situations.

The fundamental positions are given in the first form, Siu Nim Tau (Young Idea), where we understand the actions relative to a stationary partner – directly in front of us. These ideas are then expanded upon and added to, in the second form, Cham Kiu (Seeking or Crossing the Bridge), where pivoting, tracking, stepping and kicking are introduced, along with the simultaneous use of both hands, leading to the understanding of how to track down and fight a mobile enemy.

Drills like Daan Chi Sau (Single Sticking-hands Exercise), Laap Sau (Deflecting-hands Exercise) and Chi Sau then allow us to progressively explore all the possible combinations and varieties of technique, whilst in full motion. This systematic learning process gives practitioners easily understandable targets to aim at. As each level is absorbed it is then integrated and expanded upon.

person uses Fook Sau to dispel the forward pressure of the Taan Sau by sending it inwards and forwards using the whole forearm to create a subduing effect (pressed down and across) on the Taan Sau. You should attempt to position your elbow by the wrist of you partner's Taan Sau, the emphasis being on the Fook Sau's elbow not only pointing to the floor but also inwards to cover and protect the central axis.

Fook Sau concept is central to Wing Chun theory and underlies a great many of the ideas used including punching. This importance is underlined in Siu Nim Tau form by how often it is demonstrated and practised (actually and conceptually).

Pic. 16a   Pic. 16b

Bong Sau

Bong Sau comes from the word meaning the upper arm bone (or the corresponding bone in the wing of a bird, hence the common mistranslation, 'wing arm'). We are using the end of this bone (the elbow) to control an incoming force. When your Taan Sau or other action is prevented from going forwards to its intended target, the forearm relaxes and rotates – allowing the elbow to flip up by revolving around the obstruction. The Bong Sau can now take over and continue down the original line towards the opponent's central axis. If the elbow is stopped, the shoulder can take over. Alternatively, it can change back to Taan Sau, with a shift of stance (as in Daan Chi Sau with a step). Unlike most other actions, Bong Sau will not work going backwards.

Pic. 17a   Pic. 17b

Bong Sau is overused by many Wing Chun practitioners; it is only shown once on each side in Siu Nim Tau, whereas Fook Sau is shown specifically three times in the first section of Siu Nim Tau form and many other times conceptually. There are only three reasons for ever performing Bong Sau:

1. Your punching hand has been taken off its intended line towards the central axis by an on target defence – the elbow then takes up the line and continues down the original path, creating Bong Sau. If the elbow is trapped, then the shoulder can take over.

2. Your arms are down by your side (hands lower than your elbows) and someone throws an attack at you. You

lift your elbow to intercept, as it is closer to the attack than the hand and your forearm creates a shield as it is drawn across the line.

3. Your hand or wrist is pulled or someone attempts to drag you by the arm, possibly trying to hit you at the same time. Bong Sau is used to dissipate the force and redirect your energy into the attacker. It will also make it more difficult to hold onto your arm. Bong Sau should cover any incoming attacks. If the punch is low, Lan Sau (Barrier-arm Deflection) can be used here as an alternative.

Primarily using the three actions of Taan, Fook and Bong Sau, the Wing Chun practitioner aims to achieve a position of superior strength and angle with every single move. During any defence, attack, footwork-step or posture shift, the central axis line must be controlled, thus maintaining the opponent's disadvantage and forcing them to defend from a poor angle and attack down a longer path.

In training, each move can be treated as an individual step and potential choices can be analysed in simple stages. Once the best option is selected, the appropriate responses can then be drilled in and joined up into a string of individual techniques that flow from one into another. The teaching of correct positioning and range can be difficult; a clear understanding of posture, hand shapes and the central axis line needs to be gained first, then through gradual experimentation in drills such as Chi Sau and then fighting practise, positioning can be properly understood.

The Five Basic Footwork Types

Footwork in Wing Chun is less confusing if we stick with a few ground rules. Keeping it simple makes all the possible variations and interpretations easy to categorise and practise. This is not to say that these are the only ways that we can step but if we stay within these techniques, we ought to be able to deal with most situations.

1. Stepping forward to attack. This is initially taught as stepping in a straight line into the enemy's central axis. Think of stepping to the apex of an equilateral triangle and bringing the rear foot forward to follow the stance. Keep the rear heel on the floor as much as possible, to maintain a solid connection to the ground (see following structure test). Tuck the hips up and finish facing square to the opponent, with the shoulders and hips turned 100 per cent towards the target.

2. Stepping straight backwards (this is rarely used as the enemy can easily follow you, but it needs to be considered).

3. Pivoting. Keep the hips up, your weight on your heels and do not wobble about. This is used normally in response to pressure or to evade an incoming force. Rotate about the body's central axis.

4. Tui Ma, or Push Step. Used to retreat and realign under pressure, the normal stance is caused to collapse

backwards and slightly sideways. Allow your stance to be pressed and let the enemy do the work for you. The front leg needs to slide back over to cover the new central axis line, turn the front foot inward to protect the groin and rear leg and also to prevent foot sweeping. Two further variations are then possible:

a) Shuffle step: stepping again and to the same side.

b) Long stepping: stepping to the other side and changing legs accordingly.

You will need to practise both of these versions to see when they apply, it should be quite apparent and will depend on the direction of force and relative arm positions.

5. Pivoting and then collapsing. The pivot has taken place but then further pressure is applied and the pivoted position now collapses to either side as in Tui Ma. Step to the right with the right leg or to the left with the left leg.

As mentioned in 1. above, when stepping you should try to maintain contact between the heels and the ground as much as possible. This is shown in Cham Kiu form. To demonstrate why this is so, get in a forward facing stance and try to push a punch out against resistance supplied by a partner, keep your rear heel on the floor whilst doing this. Now try the same exercise again with the heel lifted off the floor using your toes or the ball of your foot to supply the pressure.

Pic.18a   Pic.18b

You will find that the first method is far stronger due to the more direct connection with the floor. Another reason for the difference is that in the second drill you are utilising the calf muscle but in the first example you activate the gluteus maximums (buttock), which is the largest and hence strongest muscle in the body. Of course, if you are out of contact you may find that you are more agile on your toes, but generally and certainly when in contact, try to keep your heels down on the floor as much as possible.

Stepping and turning should be as natural as walking to the Wing Chun practitioner. You must be able to move through stances, steps and kicks whilst maintaining perfect distance (Wong Shun Leung and Bruce Lee were both championship dancers in Hong Kong).

Understanding Tui Ma

Tui Ma is important to understand because although you will be moving backwards, you are still attempting to move closer to and gain an advantageous position over your opponent. You are not just retreating, you are being actively pushed back by a larger or stronger person but you must still maintain you structure and angle if this happens.

To better appreciate Tui Ma, stand in Yi Ji Kim Yeung Ma and hold a punch out in front of your body and then hold the fist with your other hand (keep your forearms pressed together) creating a wedge shape in front of your body, not unlike the prow of a ship. Get a partner to push this shape powerfully in towards your central axis, using both hands pressing on your clamped fists.

Pic. 19

As you feel the force of the shove in your hips, allow your stance to be pushed back on whichever side feels right. Your stance should be forced back into a different position slightly off the original line, behind the central axis line, whilst still facing with the shoulders and hips 100 per cent. If the direction is hard to feel, your partner can aid you by pressing on the forearm of one side (e.g. the right forearm), thus causing the pressure-reaction and step to happen on the opposite side (left leg).

Pic. 20

To explain the positions involved, imagine standing in the centre of a clock face with the number 12 in front of you, this is where the force comes from, 6 is behind you. As you feel the pressure pushing you back, shift your left foot to where number seven would be or right foot to where number five would be, depending on the direction of force received. After stepping back adjust your front leg up to cover the groin and rear leg. Keep facing your partner at all times and do not lift up out of your stance, let them do the work for you.

Once the Tui Ma position has been gained, stay put, and allow your partner to get back in front of you and shove you again. When the new stance is re-pushed (you imagine the clock face has shifted with you and you are now facing 12 again), you can choose to either shuffle step further round, in the same direction as before, or you can take a long step and change the direction of your footwork, swapping your feet around (Pic. 21a and b), depending on what pressure you feel. These same steps can then be introduced into a variety of the hand drills and trained to become natural. The basic rule of thumb with stepping is that if you are moving to the left, you step with your left leg and if you are moving to your right, you move with your right leg.

Pic.21a   Pic.21b

Kicking and Sweeping

Whilst spending much of the time with two feet firmly on the ground, the Wing Chun practitioner must also understand how and when to kick effectively. First though, the basic stances, steps and turns, must be learned in order to achieve a proper understanding of balance, and the dynamics of the legs and hips.

All the Wing Chun kicks are found in Cham Kiu Form and the Wooden Dummy Form, which you will learn as you progress. A brief outline of these forms is given later on. Wing Chun kicks are sometimes known as invisible or shadowless kicks. They are swift, direct and low; targets include the feet, shins, knees (front, back and side), thighs, groin and hips.

Wing Chun kicks rarely land higher than the waist. The reason for their speed and subtlety is that they work on the same principle as the hands, i.e. they usually travel straight to the target without needing to be chambered or drawn back first.

Pic. 22

Kicking from a pivot or Laap Sau

When kicking we need to know what to kick at: The simple answer is to kick at the nearest target with your closest foot. The power of the kick comes from acceleration of the leg and from pushing up from the ground, in this way, any recoil is sent back into the stance. If you kick downwards, any forceful collision can disrupt your posture and cause imbalance.

Pic. 23

Using a stamp when pulled in

If the enemy is out of striking range a sharp tug can bring them (or you) into kicking distance, it will also put the opponent's weight onto the nearest limb, making it a better target as it supports the body's weight. If there is any doubt or instability in the situation, keep your feet firmly on the ground and continue to control with the arms. Sometimes kicks will be the result of exaggerated footwork manoeuvres or hand techniques such as Laap Sau, again this makes them difficult to detect (Pic. 22).

If the posture is disrupted a kick can be used to right the situation. If the posture is broken backwards a lifting front kick can be employed, if you are out-flanked a sidekick may be appropriate. A sidekick is also a useful way to free off some arm locks. If you are pulled in, stamping on the enemy's instep is effective (Pic. 23).

Defending Against Kicks

Prevention of and defence against kicks can be achieved in several different ways; first comes proximity and pressure. Many fighters do not feel comfortable with the range that the Wing Chun practitioner employs and certainly cannot kick effectively whilst being relentlessly punched in the face. If the opponent attempts to regain distance, simply chase them back using the idea of Hoi Sung.

'Kick a kicker,' is another phrase that springs to mind here. In other words, if an opponent attempts to kick you from close range, pick your own lead leg up, preventing it being trapped against the ground and kick the supporting leg (or the kicking leg) of your opponent away (Pic. 24 a and b).

Pic.24a   Pic.24b
Kicking the supporting leg when receiving a round kick

Other equally effective defences are the use of Soh Sau (Pressing-palm Deflection) or Gaan Sau (Splitting-hand Deflection) to cover the lower areas, or simply apply downward pressure to the arm as the foot leaves the ground. This has an unbalancing effect causing the foot to be quickly put back onto the ground.

If an opponent performs a foot sweep on your leg it needs to be able to return to centre, in the same way that a hand would, and immediately re-attack them. Often a kick can be used in conjunction with the hands either as a trip, a distraction technique or as a method of creating an off-centre force in the hands.

These skills can be practised in Chi Geuk (Sticking-legs Exercise) or even in combination with Chi Sau, but care must be taken to ensure that these skills are practised under controlled conditions, heavy kicks to vulnerable parts such as the knees are dangerous (which is the whole point). Also, if you always kick in Chi Sau, there will be a tendency to neglect training the hands.

Solo Forms

A form is a pre set sequence of movements laid down to aid the correct passing on of kung fu. The form contains many movements, theories, structures and ideas. Correct training in the forms also helps to program the neural pathways and helps the practitioner focus on salient points. It is important to learn the forms and corresponding drills and theories in sequence because movements and ideas from the Siu Nim Tau (the first form) are later expanded upon in Cham Kiu (the second form) and the others.

The six Wing Chun forms contain all of the actions and ideas central to the system. To the uninitiated it may not be apparent exactly what is going on and how much information is being passed on via the forms. There are four open hand forms, one performed against a specifically designed wooden dummy, and two weapon sets; the Luk Dim Boon Gwan (Six-and-a-half-point Long Pole) and Baat Jam Do (Eight Slashing Knives form, more commonly known as the Butterfly Knives Form).

For many people, forms involve pretending to fight one or more imaginary opponents; this is not true of Wing Chun. You cannot have a fight on your own and, as Wing Chun concerns itself with concepts, as opposed to specific techniques, this thinking will restrict understanding of the system. It is more useful to keep the interpretation of the forms conceptual and broad, than to tie every movement down with a specific, unchangeable purpose. From simple concepts spring a wealth of ideas and techniques. The same is not true for the reverse.

The forms have been designed in an abstract way to prevent students becoming trapped in them. Provided the essential ideas are listened to, you can express your skill in any way you like. The forms are not a path of restriction but one toward freedom and self expression.

Siu Nim Tau

The first form is called Siu Nim Tau, meaning young idea (personally, it also reminds me that the devil is in the detail). This form is the seed from which the whole system will grow. As a tree needs strong roots to hold it up, so the first form and all the concepts held within it, must be fully understood in order for a student to progress successfully. Wong Shun Leung described Siu Nim Tau as being like learning the alphabet of Wing Chun. You will need to learn it thoroughly before you move on to Cham Kiu where you begin to blend ideas together to make the equivalent of Wing Chun words and sentences. The form is illustrated in detail at the back of this book.

The form is split into three sections with a different emphasis on each, but the overall aim is to achieve a good stance, structure and the idea of Lat Sau Jik Chung, with relaxed arms that can act independently from the trunk of the body. Many of the movements are performed on one arm at a time, whilst the other arm is kept isolated in the ready position. Siu Nim Tau contains reference points for all the basic techniques, so make sure you get it right from the outset.

The opening shows us how to find the correct stance, defines the centre line and demonstrates the centre punch. This is also the correct order of importance: Stance, centre, and attack.

The first section introduces the central idea of structure and trains us to develop the muscles and joints of the shoulder, arm and wrist in the proper way, without involving excessive movement or tension. The springy force of Taan Sau, Fook Sau and Wu Sau are also introduced. This section should be performed very slowly and deliberately, with all movement driven from the elbow. The section closes with Paak Sau (Slapping-hand Deflection), Jing Jeung (Standing-palm Strike) and Huen Sau (Rolling-wrist Deflection), which develops and stretches the muscles of the forearm.

The second section teaches the general concept of recovery. Variants of Soh (Gum) Sau (Pressing-palm Deflection) are shown and a method for recovering from a bear hug from behind. Lan Sau, Fak Sau (Whisking/Whipping-hand Attack), Jam Sau (Sinking-arm Deflection), Jat Sau (Jerking/Dragging-hand Deflection) and Biu Sau (Spearing-hand Attack) are introduced. Mostly, both arms perform the same move on opposing sides of the body. This has a balancing effect making excessive body movements less likely for the beginner. The section finishes with a downward and upward pressing action driven from the shoulders. This reminds us that even if the arms are extended – the hand can still travel directly to the target, without first drawing the arms back to the body. This section of the form should be performed briskly.

The third section describes basic shapes, teaching us how to flow simply from one position to the next. It opens with Paak Sau, Waang Jeung (Lying-palm Strike) and Huen Sau, going on to demonstrate Taan Sau applications with Jam Sau, Gaan Sau, Huen Sau and Che Jeung (Descending-palm Strike), Bong Sau with Taan Sau and Dai Jeung (Lifting-palm Deflection), then finally, two arms working together to recover from a compromised position. This section should be practised with an emphasis on correct positions and use of elbow energy. The form closes with several punches and Huen Sau.

Pic. 25

Cham Kiu

After having learned how to understand the various ideas, attacks and counters against a stationary target, the second form Cham Kiu (searching for, or crossing the bridge) teaches us how to move our bodies in order to track and fight a mobile opponent, whilst preserving the skills learnt in Siu Nim Tau. Again the form can be split into three sections, making it easier to understand, but the purpose of each section is not so specific.

Generally the first section teaches Pei Jaang (Hacking Elbow), turning on the spot and Cham Kiu Fook Sau. Jeet Sau (Arm Wrenching) is followed by a demonstration of how best to hit a moving target. Then the Bong Sau is shown in contact (Yi Bong Sau

– In Contact or Shifting Bong Sau). The change from Bong Sau to Lan Sau with correct elbow positioning is also introduced. Fak Sau follows with Jat Sau elbow used to recover an open line.

Pic. 26

The second section begins with a turn to 90 degrees with Lan Sau, and introduces Dang Geuk (Ascending Kick). Lan Sau is kept low to prevent an opponent using it to push against us or pull us out of position. Forward stepping footwork is demonstrated, the centre line is at 90 degrees to the direction in which you are stepping. Bong Sau is now demonstrated out of contact (Paau Bong Sau). The Chau Kuen (Whipping Punch) is travelling straight to the target at approximately chest height and not uppercutting in the classical Western boxing way, but the elbow may be simultaneously covering an attack. Finally Yi Ying Sau (Shape-Recovering Hand) shows us how to salvage a poor position without being hit.

The third section shows us the front kick, forward footwork, the step back and backward/side kick. Two separate methods of close body control are demonstrated using the Dai Bong (Low Bong Sau), pushing from the stance and Soh Sau to cover the lower gates against kicks via the arms. Finally punching to cover an exposed flank is demonstrated. The overall theme of Cham Kiu is tracking and gaining contact with a mobile enemy, then crossing over the bridge to their centre by virtue of correct positioning and angle.

Muk Yan Jong

Wooden dummy training forms an intrinsic part of the Wing Chun system. Literally translated Muk Yan Jong means 'a stake used as a dummy'. Other styles of kung fu use dummies to practise against but the Wing Chun dummy and its form is specifically designed to practise and improve Wing Chun skills. The form has undergone many changes throughout its history; originally it consisted of 140 movements. Grandmaster Yip Man thought this number too numerous and reduced them to 108 (considered a lucky number by Chinese people). Later though he decided that some vital parts were missing and increased the amount to 116 techniques where it is generally accepted to remain to this day (although there are many different versions of this form).

Pic. 27

Wong Shun Leung practising on a dummy

Training in the Wooden Dummy Form will improve many aspects of skill, especially your ability to recover from the errors that we inevitably make in fighting. Another useful effect of dummy training is that the pre-set angles of the arms will help to perfect the delivery of techniques and hone the angle of attack.

It is of course possible to strike and kick the dummy with considerably more force than you could safely use against a training partner. It must however be pointed out that the purpose of the wooden dummy is not to harden the arms or hands. The practitioner should not bash themselves recklessly into the arms. Lastly, the dummy form contains many kicks, trips, traps and throws as well as combination movements not previously seen in the solo forms.

Biu Ji

The name and concept of Biu Ji, the so-called mysterious third form of Wing Chun, is derived from the idiom about looking beyond the finger pointing at the moon (look at the moon, not the finger!). The secrecy surrounding it stems from the fact that it is often only taught to loyal students who have shown themselves to be capable of a high level of development, both through the physical system and on a personal level.

Before learning Biu Ji a student must have absorbed all the concepts from Siu Nim Tau, Cham Kiu, and up until the fourth section of Muk Yan Jong. Many of the moves contradict ideas that we have been taught up until this point in our training.

Pic. 28

The form teaches us to think outside the box when necessary. It contains many ideas, including ways of minimising one's losses if you have been hit, injured or made a bad mistake during a fight. Methods are also given for cutting back to the centre after an error and escapes when leverage or centre is lost.

For these reasons it is also known as the emergency or desperation form. This is why it should not be shown too early in a person's training. It is better to learn not to make mistakes, than to find ways of correcting them after they have been made.

Luk Dim Boon Gwan

The first of the Weapon Sets, Luk Dim Boon Gwan, literally translates as Six-and-a-half-point-long Pole. This form is believed to have been introduced around the time of the Red Junk opera troop. It is a short form and introduces the basic parries and attacks; there are only six and a half techniques, hence the name. Practising the pole form correctly will develop great strength in the wrists and stance.

It is possible to practise sticking pole techniques with a partner; the idea is to stick to the end of the partner's pole maintaining a strong position and range until a strike becomes available. This skill is not unlike fencing. When an opening becomes available, trap the pole, strike through or slide down the other pole to attack the hands.

Pole practice teaches new footwork and positioning, so it is very useful as a training method. It is also possible to train with a pole against butterfly knives.

Pic. 29

Wong Shun Leung training knives vs pole

Baat Jaam Do

The second Weapon Set, Baat Jaam Do (Eight Slashing Knives), clearly dates to a time when kung fu skills were a matter of life and death. Despite popular belief, open hand fighting is practically useless against a skilled, armed warrior.

The Baat Jaam Do is also known as the Butterfly Knives Form because of the appearance of the blades when crossed. The form is in eight sections demonstrating the various defensive and attacking manoeuvres.

The knives are used as an extension of the hand shapes and many of the common techniques can be performed with knives. When fighting the aim is to attack the opponent's weapon hands first. The prong on the guard can be used to trap a weapon.

In the present day, practice with swords and pole could be seen as obsolete, however this form is very useful, supplying a different type of footwork and positioning. The weight and balance of the blades is also a very effective way of training for posture and wrist strength. Training with weapons will also give a greater perception of threat and hence change the way that you move. It is also important to learn the entire system (even if you do not utilise all of the techniques yourself), in order that you can eventually pass it on, in its entirety, to others. They may well favour some of the ideas that you have rejected.

Pic. 30

Wong Shun Leung with the knives

The Wing Chun Drills

The Wing Chun system has many unique drills. They are often performed in contact, and are frequently cyclic, to allow simple repetitions and variations. The purpose of these drills is to program an appropriate response into the body's neural system.

Some of the drills have a set pattern of movements but techniques always need to be responsive and not anticipated. To this end once the basic drills have been understood, they can be varied according to a specific concept. Eventually drills should blend in with, and become an integral part of Chi Sau and fighting practice.

Daan Chi Sau

The basic ideas of Taan, Bong, Fook, and Jam Sau, as well as correct palm strike, punching, stance and facing are all nicely contained in the Daan Chi Sau (Single-Sticking hands) drill. Start from a square on position, deliberately out of range for safety's sake (this also allows for full extension of technique), with one person in Taan Sau and the other in a corresponding Fook Sau.

Pic.31

The person in Taan Sau should fire a relaxed but springy Jing Jeung, aiming at the chin area of their partner. Maintain your squareness – do not push the shoulder forward, reach in or lean. Maintain good structure and springy pressure throughout the entire action. Allow the attack to recoil in a natural way, leaving it in a suitable position to apply Bong Sau if needed, not straight and stiff but elastic and with a subtle forward intention. If the palm strike is too low there is no perception of threat. If there is no threat, there is no need to deflect – just trade with a punch to the face.

The opponent keeps a relaxed and springy Fook Sau, with a slight pressure from the whole forearm toward the centre of their partner. When the palm strike is sent forward, the pressure causes Jam Sau to be applied with the elbow. Jam Sau is possible here (using the elbow moving diagonally towards the central axis) because the

Fook Sau elbow is relaxed, slightly forward and out initially. Because the elbow and not the wrist has been used to deflect the palm, the intercepting arm should now be nicely lined up to attack back. The pressure is still slightly maintained on the elbow to match the springy force of the attacking hand.

Pic. 32

The initial defender now has the line to re-attack and punches (keeping the elbow down and driving it forwards) into the chest area, whilst maintaining good structure. If this punch is weak or the elbow position is out or rising, you can simply defend by punching back to the face.

Pic. 33

The initial attacker now needs to defend their position by applying Bong Sau to control the incoming elbow (with the force of the Bong Sau elbow pointing to the centre), whilst still maintaining pressure from the stance to control the action. Bong Sau happens because the pressure on the arm forces the hand off-centre, allowing the elbow to take over the original line of attack.

Pic. 34

The arms both now return to the starting position and the process repeats itself. Remember that each action causes a response triggered by feeling. The palm strike initiates a Jam Sau and then the punch initiates a Bong Sau: you must keep this in mind when training. Breaking up the rhythm and changing the feel of the attacks will challenge the partner to react according to sensitivity, as opposed to pre-empting the next move. Naturally, this drill needs to be trained on both arms and both partners must practise each role.

Note: if you constantly hug the centre with your elbows in any sticking hands drill, neither you nor your partner will be able to train freely (meet what comes). You will develop defensive thinking; you will also get very sore arms and rounded shoulders. Overuse of or leading with the shoulders is very common and this can be used as an easy guide as to what someone is going to do next. Using the shoulders excessively also allows you to be controlled very easily, due to the extra strength and leverage that this necessitates. If you allow your arms to relax and let your elbows drift out a bit, you will then be able to train more freely, and practise bringing them in when they are needed. If your elbows are not defending the centre, you can then keep your forearms lined up to hit, this encourages assertive thinking.

Daan Chi Sau with a Step

Start from a square position, with one person in Taan Sau and the other in a corresponding Fook Sau. As with the Single Sticking-hands drill, the person in Taan Sau steps forward, straight in, attacking with a relaxed but springy palm strike, aimed at the chin area of their partner. Think of stepping to the apex of an equilateral triangle, straight down the centre. The line that joins your two feet in the Yi Ji Kim Yeung Ma is the base of the triangle.

Pic. 35

The opponent's Fook Sau arm receives the pressure of the palm strike and sinks to Jam Sau while maintaining forward energy to the attacker's central axis (if the attack feels too high, you may need to control it downward to provide better structure). Pressure on the fixed elbow position forces a retreat as the hip is pressed back using Tui Ma. If left Fook Sau is being used, step back with your left leg. The right leg needs to adjust up to achieve a good strong stance and protect the groin and rear leg (as in Cham Kiu).

Pic. 36

The partner now has the line and angle to re-attack straight back in with a step and punch to the chest area. As an option, at this point it is also possible to engage in Chi Geuk, which will be examined at the end of this section.

The initial attacker now needs to adjust position by shuffle stepping to a short Taan Sau (as in Siu Nim Tau after third section Jam Sau) and punch, by moving the elbow and forearm to a position of superior strength (Pic. 37). As an option, it is also possible to engage in Chi Geuk at this point.

Pic. 37

Pic.38a

Pic.38b

Alternatively, if the incoming punch is too strong or well positioned, move your front foot sideward to become your new back foot (your rear foot adjusts up to be on Cham Kiu line, keeping the lead leg rotated in). This is referred to as 'Long Stepping'. As this happens apply Bong Sau (as in Cham Kiu second section Paau Bong) to control the incoming elbow with your own. Maintain a pressure from your Bong Sau, across the enemy's stance to disrupt and bounce out their forward motion.

Pic. 39

Remember, during this and other stepping drills never reach out in order to hit. The shoulders should always remain square, down and relaxed, the elbows should stay bent and flexible. Also maintain a good structure whilst stepping; keep the hips pushed up and hold the body in balance.

Using Fook Sau Concept to Intercept Punches

This is a good training exercise to help people understand how one simple concept (Fook Sau) can be used to deal with a whole range of possible situations. When attacked with a straight punch, send both hands out, as Fook Sau, towards the enemy's centre, utilising springy force. The soft side of the arm should face the attack. One hand should go towards centre (head) and the other should give two points of contact/control. You should step either forwards or backwards (depending on the incoming force that you are intercepting) using Tui Ma, leaving hips and shoulders facing the enemy. You may need to use your arms to help push you back, or you may need to step into a weaker attack. The end position is pretty much the same, whichever way you step, relative to the enemy (100 per cent square facing shoulders and hips).

Pic. 40a

Pic. 40b

A second straight line attack is met in the same way by using the outside hand to press the centre and intercept the second attack. You may need to change footwork here but the primary aim is to shut down the attack and suppress any further movements. Only hit when correct fighting range is reached.

Pic. 41

If a hook or round punch is sent, you need to step in to the attack and shut it down before the shoulder gets forward. The step is the same movement as for a straight punch, but in the opposite direction. Think of the action of the hook as a door being briefly opened, as the door opens step inside quickly. Move in square to the shoulder/upper arm and send one hand to the head (centre) and the other near the elbow. Both of your elbows need to be bent and pointing at the floor (the depth of your forearm is equal to your margin for error). The hand that is stopping the attack needs to cross the punching arm, near the elbow, roughly at right angles. Make sure that it is your forearm that is stopping the attack and not your hand, as this will be too weak and vulnerable to damage.

Pic. 42a   Pic. 42b   Pic. 42c

If a second punch comes, you will need to turn and step into the attack and hit in the same way as before. You can use Fook Sau but Taan Sau and a punch will also work from this position. Taan Sau will change the round attack into a straight line. The alternative to this is to use the jaw as a lever and press the head (using the hand that hit initially) towards the shoulder of the next punch. This will jam the body's rotation and prevent the punch from gaining any power. It is also possible to control the elbow in the same direction, then spin the whole body round to face away from you and drag the enemy into a choke, (using them as a shield against other attackers, if they are present) or just drop them onto their backs on the ground.

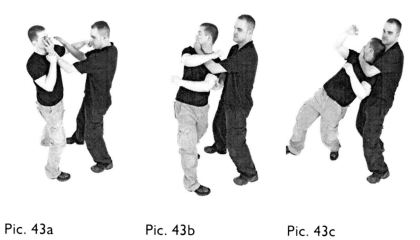

Pic. 43a   Pic. 43b   Pic. 43c

Another way of dealing with a rotating (hooking) action of this type, is to move forward and turn with the person (staying facing the target). Using the idea of Cham Kiu Fook Sau, as demonstrated in the first section of the Cham Kiu form, it is possible to hook or Laap Sau the incoming punch and allow the body's rotation to continue along it's original path but give it a slight downwards tug – helping the attacker to over-commit and pulling them off balance as you strike them back with your other hand.

Wu Sau

Any time that a hand is not performing a task, it is normally held in the Wu Sau (Guarding Hand) position. Wu Sau lies on the central axis line, covering the chin, throat or nose in case any attacks penetrate the defence. Wu Sau is also a position of readiness; the hand is primed to spring out from the centre to attack, or take on any other shape; always active, never passive.

Wu Sau and Punch:
General Turning Punch Drills

Using a punch and Wu Sau to receive punches is good for training the pivot and Wu Sau awareness. The attacking person, the one who is supplying the punches, is training to punch correctly and at full extension; they are also getting a strength and conditioning exercise for the arms and whole stance. You should push punches out hard to develop resistance.

The person receiving punches is using Wu Sau and a punch to deflect the incoming punches and re-attack. The arms must remain springy and the Wu Sau forearm should be pointing back at the enemy's centre and ready to attack. Gaining two points of contact is stronger when receiving an attack and forces the attacker to re-attack from the other hand, down a predictable line.

Pic. 44

When the next punching attack is sent out, pressing up from behind the recently landed punch, the opponent pivots to the other side (allowing the attacker to move them) and alternates the Wu Sau and punching hand, thus planting the punch over the opposite elbow and into the centre of mass. This process is then repeated. At any time the puncher can release the pressure on the punching arm and the Wu Sau hand of the opponent should shoot forward. Although in Siu Nim Tau, Wu Sau is moving backwards, in reality it is trying to spring forwards and the arm is lined up to attack.

Pic. 45

At random times the puncher can grab an arm and try to pull the defender off balance – the defender should use their stance to realign their attack, creating a Lan Sau (like at the start of the second section of Cham Kiu) to drive forward and destabilise the person attempting to pull.

Pic. 46

Alternatively the puncher can randomly push or shove the defender, attempting to uproot their stance and drive them back. This push should force the stance pivot to collapse into Tui Ma and retreat into the 7 or 5 o'clock position. Wu Sau is again constantly ready and on line, to spring forward into attack or cover the next move. This drill or concept can then easily be translated into Chi Sau.

Pic. 47

If the attacker fails to attack down the line behind the recently landed punch and it slips by close to the other side of the fist, then the last punch is converted into Gaan Sau, scooping the punch out of the way and redirecting the attacker's force (Pic. 48). If the attack is well wide of the last punch, then Fook Sau and punch would be the appropriate response (Pic. 49).

Pic. 48a   Pic. 48b   Pic. 48c

Pic. 49

Using the concept of Fook Sau to intercept a hook

Many of the actions of Wing Chun can be drilled repetitively in the same way as this drill, by using turning as a response to straight punches. Once the initial ideas have been drilled in, it is then possible to start varying and mixing up the actions used as a defence, to get used to improvising under pressure

These drills help students to understand how to subdue or suppress an attack or follow up with the same or a different hand: This is similar to the way that the third section of Siu Nim Tau shows us how to flow from one position to the next. In fact it is not difficult to fit most of these (Siu Nim Tau third section) actions in with this drill.

You can also train to simply intercept and cut across punches with your own punches using the Fook Sau concept. Ultimately, you will be applying these ideas whilst attempting to go forwards to shut down an attack but you might equally work them going backwards.

Wu Sau and Punch: General Retreat Drills

This is a retreat drill utilising a forward stepping punching attack, and the Tui Ma in action, as opposed to a stationary pivot as above.

Working against stepping forward punches, change sides as you retreat alternately to 5 or 7 o'clock. If the punches are too high, make sure that Wu Sau/Jam Sau controls the height of incoming punches. Drag them down, using the sinking elbow, to a good structural position (the same technique can be applied for the above, static drill). It is possible to add a couple of punches on to the end of the Jam Sau technique, once you are settled into your stances, and still end up in the same place – hips and shoulders facing your opponent, ready to intercept the next incoming punch.

Pic. 50a   Pic. 50b

When attacking, you can step forwards maintaining the same lead leg, or you can alternate legs. Press your punches out using you step to gain power. This will help the defender feel the pressure driving their elbow/hip back into the 'collapsing' Tui Ma.

Again, many of the actions of Wing Chun can be drilled repetitively in the same way, in response to stepping punches. Once the initial ideas have been drilled in, it is then possible to start varying and mixing up the actions.

Pic. 51a   Pic. 51b

Laap Sau and Paak Sau

Although Laap Sau and Paak Sau are techniques of attack; they can also be used to control and to defend. It is essential for the practitioner to spend plenty of time with these ideas and to get familiar with the variety of ways in which they can be used. Literally translated Laap Sau means deflecting or warding off hands, Paak Sau means slapping hand.

Pic. 52a   Pic. 52b   Pic. 52c

Laap Sau technique, with a punch

Laap Sau

Laap Sau is often used when the lead arm is in contact with the opponent's limb, but they are slightly out of range. The arm is given a short, sharp tug. At the same time, an attack is launched from the other hand. The opponent's arm is pulled out of the way, and they are pulled onto the attack (Pic. 52a, b and c).

Laap Sau Drill

Laap Sau drill is cyclic; one person performs a Laap Sau technique with a punch, the partner maintains the centre using Bong Sau and Wu Sau. The opponent then performs Laap Sau and punches with their Bong Sau hand. The original attacker then utilises Bong Sau. This process is then repeated (Pic. 53a, b, c, d and e).

Pic. 53a   Pic. 53b   Pic. 53c

Pic. 53d   Pic. 53e

Laap Sau drill

A change of sides can be obtained if the defender, using the hand of his Bong Sau arm, grasps and pulls the arm that has just performed Laap Sau on him. (Pic. 54a b and c).

It is important to remain relaxed throughout the drill. You must take care not to over-commit with either Bong Sau or the punch and be mindful of where the centre is at all times. When performing Laap Sau, it is good to vary the speed and strength of your technique. This will test your partner's Bong Sau. It is easy to devise variations and interruptions to the Laap Sau drill. These changes will encourage improvisation and enable the development of a more rounded skill. Wu Sau should be on the centre and held back near the shoulder to prevent it getting trapped.

Pic. 54a   Pic. 54b   Pic. 54c

Laap Sau drill, showing a change of sides

Variations on Laap Sau Drill

Normally Laap Sau will be used when you are slightly out of range, to draw the enemy back in and is often employed after using Bong Sau defensively. As a drill, Laap Sau is very good for developing flow and helps you to remain relaxed whilst under pressure. It is also excellent for teaching you that the elbow is where we have to emphasise our control once the hands are otherwise occupied. Laap Sau drill also reminds us that after receiving an attack we must immediately attack back.

Laap Sau Drill 1

Begin facing each other, with crossed Mun Sau positions: one person Laaps and punches, pulling the Laap slightly across the centre. The defender then uses Wu Sau, sending it forward down the centre. The original attacker then makes contact with the Wu Sau and Laaps and punches again. Pulling the Laap Sau slightly over the centre will make defending more difficult and exaggerate responses, making them more easy to deal with.

Laap Sau Drill 2

From the Laap Sau drill one person attacks using the Fook Sau concept from the first section in Cham Kiu and Paak Sau. The Fook Sau comes off the Bong Sau that you have just made and Paak Sau comes off your Wu Sau hand, you turn the hips back to face your partner and step straight into their stance as you attack.

In the initial stages of this drill, the easiest way to deal with this attack is to seal the centre with your Wu Sau (which was your last punch) and then attempt to use Jat Sau and punch back.

Pic. 55a

Pic. 55b

Pic. 55c

Pic. 55d

Laap Sau Drill 3

From the Laap Sau drill one person attacks with Fook Sau and Paak Sau as above. Depending on the pressure received from the initial Paak Sau, you can respond with Paak Sau or a reciprocal Taan Sau and punch on a pivot. The hand that was controlling the Bong Sau may become the Taan Sau (if the Paak Sau pressure is downwards or not across the body too much). In this case, your Taan Sau will end up over and outside of the attacking punch.

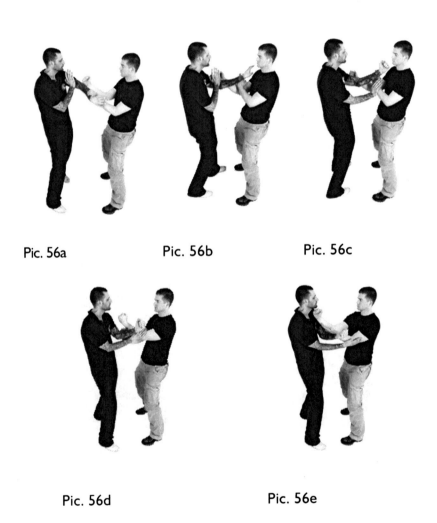

Pic. 56a   Pic. 56b   Pic. 56c

Pic. 56d   Pic. 56e

Laap Sau Drill 4

From the Laap Sau drill one person moves as if to punch but instead, shoves their partner's Bong Sau elbow and tries to jam it against their body or push them back with it.

Using good body structure and sensitivity, the defender will need to employ a Taan Sau and punch in order to defend in conjunction with the Tui Ma to avoid being trapped up or bundled over. The direction of the step will be dependent on the direction and force of the shove.

Pic. 57a   Pic. 57b

Both parties can then square their footwork back up by using Bong Sau; get back into the Laap Sau drill and repeat the exercise at will

Laap Sau Drill 5

From the Laap Sau drill one person attacks by changing the punching hand into Paak Sau and striking into the chest area with the hand that has just performed the Laap. This is excellent as a test for your partner's Wu Sau position. If you have kept your Wu Sau going forward along the central axis, with the elbow down, you will be able to slip it out alongside the attacking arm and disperse it using the action of Taan Sau (Pic. 58a, b and c).

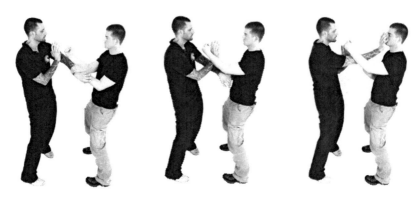

Pic. 58a   Pic. 58b   Pic. 58c

Testing Wu Sau from the Laap Sau drill

If your Wu Sau elbow is out of it's correct position (near the hip), because you have let it drift out when grabbing the wrist to Laap, your Wu Sau arm will be crushed down and you will be hit. Either that or you will be struck from beneath your grabbing arm. (Pic. 59 a and b).

Pic. 59a   Pic. 59b

Wu Sau elbow being drawn out of position by grabbing across,
instead of going forwards along the central axis line

Paak Sau

Paak Sau is derived from the Chinese verb to clap; it is a short percussive palm strike toward the centre. Paak Sau can be used as a non-committal deflection; it can also be used to control or move a limb to facilitate an attack from the other hand. Normally the attack would be launched from the lead (closest) hand.

Paak Sau Drill

Start by working off an initial attack of three stationary, full extension Wing Chun punches. Use three alternating Paak Saus to defend – aim the hands to the central axis line and use a slight pivot to achieve the angle. Think of the Paak Sau as deflecting/suppressing the incoming attacks and making follow-up attacks more difficult and predictable. Then, vary the rhythm to 1: Paak, 2: Paak, 3: Paak and 4: punch.

Pic. 60a

Pic. 60b

Pic. 60c

Pic. 60d

Using this same Paak Sau drill we can now learn to use the idea against a punching attack that is moving forward or retreating. Utilise either the shuffle step or long step to develop entry timing and to access different sides or train alternative footwork (as given in Single Sticking-hands with a step). Step in with same hand (punching) and same leg; try to get your entry step to cut through the enemy's stance. Get your knee close to the opposite knee (your left to your enemy's right, across their stance) if possible, for maximum disruptive effect. Paak Sau should be controlling near the elbow.

Pic. 61a

Pic. 61b

Pic. 61c

Pic. 61d

When using this concept going forwards against a retreating puncher, you should close down the attack within a couple of steps. Send the Paak Sau in towards the central axis line and move forward faster than they can retreat, as if striking into the enemies chin/throat area. As soon as a suitable contact and range are achieved you should be *actually* hitting.

Alternatively, after Paak Sau has passed the arm, over-commit the action to just beyond the central axis line with the lead hand. This will predict the second attack down a predefined path. Cut out following attacks with your lead hand using the same concept until your own attack line becomes apparent. You can use this drill to understand that it is always a good idea to leave your lead hand forward and use Jat Sau, Fook Sau, Cham Kiu Fook Sau or Laap Sau.

Pic. 62a   Pic. 62b   Pic. 62c

It is good practice not to switch hands every time with the enemy if this is not necessary. Whilst your hand is pressing the centre or in his face, the onus is on him to deal with or get around it, thus forcing him to take a longer route.

Now try varying the attack to a boxing Jab and Cross (a common attacking manoeuvre) and use the same over-committed defence to close down the attacks. Also vary this drill with a shove and punch, a common prelude to further violence, or a pressing punch, which is often used to set a person up for a big hit. Other variations that can be used for this drill include using Paak and Mun Sau, firstly off a Jab and then Jab – Cross combination. Alternatively, you can work with a Paak Sau to get beyond the Jab and then work Paak or Laap Sau on the Cross.

This idea works well because the pressure on the lead arm caused by Paak Sau (or more precisely the pressure being suddenly removed as the next attack is launched), creates an off-centre second attack. To understand this more clearly get a partner to hold out a punch and apply pressure to it near the elbow, as a Paak Sau would. You should be facing the target with square shoulders and hips. Then get your partner to throw another punch directly at you.

As you feel the punch being unleashed, release the pressure on the arm and make a small footwork adjustment shift, at the same time change hands to cover the outside of the next arm. You should end up facing your partner from the opposite side, having shifted through ninety degrees relative to them. If you manage this with appropriate timing, you will not get punched on the nose.

Pic. 63a   Pic. 63b

This same idea can be used in conjunction with Huen Sau, against a fighting guard. When Jam Sau is used to deflect an incoming punch, Huen Sau can be quickly employed to fling the attack away, creating an off-centre force in the attackers body and throwing the second punch slightly off target. The slight destabilising effect gives you a little more time to find the correct position on the flank. You need to immediately shut down the next attack using Jam Sau, in order to gain Wing Chun range.

Pic. 64a   Pic. 64b   Pic. 64c

Another way of dealing with a guard or two hands coming forward is to use a technique known as the 'Bow and Arrow' (actually Cham Kiu Fook Sau and Laan Sau together)

Pic. 65a   Pic. 65b   Pic. 65c

Variations on Paak Sau Drill

Paak Sau Drill 1: Paak Laap

Starting from facing stances, both in one foot forward and crossed Mun Sau positions, one person attacks using Paak Sau and punch. The other person responds using Paak Sau. When the original attackers punch is intercepted with Paak Sau they then employ the Under-Laap (Laap Sau from under the arm) and continue their attack. If they catch the rear Wu Sau with Fak Sau they can Laap this also; Paak is actually preferable in this last action because the hand that was Fak Sau is far nearer the face. So, the hand that was used initially for Under-Laap, is used to Paak your partner's Wu Sau as you punch.

Pic. 66a

Pic. 66b

Pic. 66c

Pic. 66d

Paak Sau Drill 2: Paak Punch

Starting as above, when the Paak and punch is intercepted with Paak Sau, continue to attack with a second punch. The opponent then Paaks (or slaps) the next attack over and down to trap the arms and punches simultaneously.

Pic. 67a
Pic. 67b

Pic. 67c
Pic. 67d

Paak Sau Drill 3

Starting as above but after intercepting the first attack with Paak, leave the same hand forward and intercept the following punch with Cham kiu Fook Sau and then either Laap down to cover the next attack and hit or Paak and hit again. Paak is better as the hand that is closest is used to hit.

Pic. 68a   Pic. 68b

Pic. 68c

Paak Sau Drill 4

After initial interception with Paak Sau leave the hand forward and Laap and punch the next attack. Drag the Laap Sau across and down over the other arm to trap and prevent further attacks.

Pic. 69a

Pic. 69b

Pic. 69c

Pic. 69d

Paak Sau Drill 5

Starting as above, when Paak and punch is intercepted with Paak Sau, continue to attack with Taan Sau and a second punch. You may need to draw the Taan Sau back and hit off what was the Paak Sau hand. This will train you to exploit the opposite side of the body and be more assertive in your occupation of the centre.

Pic. 70a

Pic. 70b

Pic. 70c

After a while of using Laap Sau and Paak Sau drills you should be able to start blending them together, with the ultimate aim of being able to flow between Chi Sau, Laap Sau and Paak Sau at will or as the situation dictates. This will help vastly with your ability to flow and hopefully prevent you from habitually throwing out Wu Sau or Mun Sau, as the result of a panic reflex, only to find that it ends up jammed forcefully on the centre.

Chi Sau: The Wing Chun Laboratory

Chi Sau is one of the reasons why Wing Chun is different. No other martial arts have a training exercise to equal the speed at which extremely high levels of skill can be learned.

Tai Chi, and some other styles, practice a pushing hands drill (akin to Daan Chi Sau in Wing Chun). This exercise only involves the use of one hand or side at a time and is teaching a different skill. The unique exercise of Chi Sau teaches us to be sensitive to the movements of our opponent and to react in accordance with exactly what is happening.

We are always very aware of where our hands are relative to our bodies. (We rarely hit ourselves accidentally.) If our arms are in contact with the opponent's, we know instinctively where our opponent is, so it becomes more simple to stop them from hitting us.

The forearms, hands and fingers are very sensitive to movement and can be taught control in a very subtle way. When we pick up a delicate object we do not use the same force necessary to pick up, for instance, a sack of potatoes. We only grip as firmly as we need to, if something slips, feedback through the nervous system automatically tells us to grip more firmly or change our position. Chi Sau operates largely on this subconscious level.

The purpose of drills like Chi Sau is to provide a learning link between the forms and fighting. It quickly teaches us how to apply the random techniques of free fighting in an environment of safety and learning. Risk of injury is slight as Chi Sau is a learning process and not a fight. For this reason we can liken Chi Sau to testing our skills under laboratory conditions as opposed to the rough road test of real fighting practice.

Learning research has shown that random practice is far more effective than practising prearranged sets of movements. Drills are learned in Chi Sau but it is also used to experiment and ad lib. You never know what to expect, and must learn to feel attacks in order to defend correctly. There is also little evidence that the conditions, under which a skill is learned, need to replicate those in which they will eventually be used. This means that you don't need to fight whilst practising Chi Sau, in order to learn effective fighting skill.

During Chi Sau practice the mind must be focused and unclouded. The need to concentrate and be single minded clears the mind and stops us from thinking about anything else. Often training will reach the level where there is no time to think of anything at all. At this point we have to trust and rely on our body's automatic systems, switching off the conscious mind. Elite level athletes have always known of the need for a relaxed body and concentrated mind (a state often referred to as 'being in the zone').

Because Chi Sau is about training sensitivity it is also easy to practise with one person blindfolded. This will heighten the sensitivity in the arms, as this is all they have to rely on. If you do practise blindfolded, or with closed eyes, it is important to remember that the person with restricted vision will be able to feel where your centre is, but may not be so aware of how close you are. So keep your head back!

Different training partners will feel quite distinct, even if the same teacher has taught them. This is because of different body types, personalities, and interpretations of technique. For this reason it is a good idea to train with as many partners as possible, in this way you will gain experience of how to deal with a larger number of situations.

It is apparent that Chi Sau requires focused concentration, and considerable skill. At first this will be difficult because you will be trying to interpret a situation that is constantly changing and using actions with which you may not be familiar. To enable a student to get used to the process Daan Chi Sau is practised first.

Once these skills have been mastered, students progress to the Chi Sau Roll (Rolling-hands exercise). This introduces the basic shapes of Chi Sau; Bong, Taan, and Fook Sau, without technique, from here hand changes can be learned and the student progresses naturally onto full Chi Sau. The Chi Sau Roll is a part of full Chi Sau training, but it is also used as a neutral gear, between techniques (Pic. 71a and b).

Pic. 71a   Pic. 71b

The Chi Sau Roll

Chi Sau Roll

One of the easiest ways to learn the Chi Sau Roll, (this is also known as Poon Sau) is by breaking it into two halves. Start off by just doing it one sided, or with one arm only. As normal, you need to stand square on to your partner, making sure that you do not over reach and keep your shoulders down and back. One person is in the Fook Sau position; the other is in Taan Sau. The person in Taan Sau now rotates their arm to Bong Sau position and back again (as a result of pressure on the Fook Sau action). At the same time the other person maintains the action of Fook Sau, keeping the springy force pressing lightly towards the centre. The person with the Fook Sau may need to adjust the position of their elbow to prevent the forearm being thrown off target.

Pic. 72a　　　　　　　　　　Pic. 72b

Using half the Chi Sau Roll simplifies the learning process

Of course, there are four different ways that this drill can be trained (Fook Sau and Taan/Bong Sau on the right and left arm) and each way round should be trained equally. In fact it is better to train your non-dominant side much more than your dominant side and always to teach this side first. The reason that the forms always begin on the left hand side is that most people are right-handed. If you are left-handed you should start on your right. If you learn a new task on your non-dominant side, the skill will transfer to your dominant side without training – the same is not true in reverse. You should also practise as much as possible on your bad side, because you will never be able to choose which side you rely upon in a fight.

Once the roll has been trained and the skill suitably absorbed on all four sides of the roll, you can start to combine them. There are normally only the two ways of combining the actions in the Chi Sau Roll (you would not normally spend much time rolling with Bong and Taan Sau on both arms or two Fook Saus) and again it is best to start off and train more on your non-dominant side. If you are right sided, this means that you start off with Taan and Bong Sau on your left side and Fook Sau on your right.

Single Hand Drill in Chi Sau Roll

This drill can also be done outside of the Chi Sau Roll, just like Daan Chi Sau, as a preliminary exercise. It is a great drill because it helps you understand that: (a) You do not always have to defend using Bong Sau and Laap Sau, which involves two or more actions, and (b) Taan Sau is a smaller, stronger movement and only requires one action, even though it may not feel like the most natural defence at first.

Start from the Chi Sau Roll; remember to roll on both sides. As one person reaches the bottom of the roll (in Taan Sau position), they send out a palm strike, just as in Daan Chi Sau. The partner reacts to this threat by using Jam Sau to receive the attack. Send back a straight punch (elbow down) to the chest area of the original attacker; this punch causing a defensive reaction. The inclination here is to apply a Bong Sau – but we are now training a different action and want to utilise a short Taan Sau, like the one in Siu Nim Tau form, third section, straight after the Jam Sau. The elbow rotates inward and forward, dispersing the punch.

Pic. 73a   Pic. 73b

The roll then continues and the drill is repeated on the opposite side and from the opposite hands. You must not over-commit or over-reach your structure during any drills and you need to maintain the constant springy force. Of course it is also possible to roll in Chi Sau and then just randomly put the palm strike in, to make sure that you are both reacting appropriately to given forces and not just being robotic.

Pic. 74a

Pic. 74b

Pic. 74c

The chief aim of this drill is to develop the ability for totally independent actions (or in this case, non-action) on both sides of the body. Thus, it is absolutely essential that while the lower arm positions interact through the palm-strike/Taan Sau actions, the upper arms remain totally still, relaxed and with forward intent. In this way, we are creating the ability to simultaneously attack and defend at all times under contact conditions.

Should you detect your partner's arms collapsing, even slightly, during the cycle of exchanges, initiate an attack to further collapse their structure, or at least let them know that they are doing it – more often than not, he or she will not realise that this is happening. A predictable reaction to this drill is that a feeling akin to a 'stitch' (as one might feel in the abdomen when running) will occur in the shoulders. This is just Mother Nature's way of letting us know that we are restricting what is a very normal motion, hence the muscles will tend to slightly spasm and ache. This is temporary and easily overcome by shaking the shoulders and changing sides.

Hand Changes and Lat Sau in Chi Sau

Once a student has learned the Chi Sau Roll to develop sensitivity in the shapes, the next step towards Chi Sau is to learn how to respond when pressure is applied in various directions.

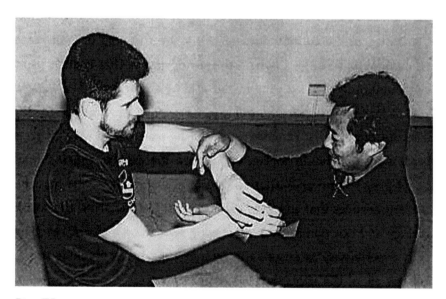

Pic. 75

Wong Shun Leung practising the Chi Sau Roll with David Peterson

Using the idea that when a hand is pushed off the centre it must return to it as smoothly and swiftly as possible, we can learn to swiftly change our hand positions in response to a very slight off-centre force.

The roll back to centre can be taught out of the Chi Sau Roll on individual hands at first but should be integrated as soon as the student is familiar with the Chi Sau Roll. The hand changes will move an arm from the inside to the outside and vice versa.

As the hands change and return to centre they must also be feeling gently towards the centre. In the early stages the practitioner must learn to react to any force that pushes the hand out or down from the centre causing the hand to roll back in and attempt to re-attack. Once this skill has been attained they must then learn to produce changes in their partner by deliberately pushing slightly off-centre, then sticking to their partner's hand as it returns to prevent being hit themselves.

It is also useful to introduce at this stage the idea of 'hand free hit centre' (Lat Sau Jik Chung – the springy force that enables us to instantaneously fill any gaps in the enemy's defence). The easiest way to learn this important skill is to have a Chi Sau partner quickly take out one hand at random times during training. As soon as your hand is free it should spring, or fall into the centre, there should be no preparation or hesitation. Here, as always, it is vital that the student ensures that any forward movement of the arms is relaxed, springy and not committed i.e. staying square on and not reaching in. It is quite easy to ensure this by interrupting, or blocking some, but not all, of the shots that fall into the centre.

Defending in Chi Sau is a matter of counter attacking, maintaining a superior position and controlling the central axis line; it is important to redirect the opponent's attack and not to use excessive force in controlling it. If force is used, a skilled opponent will feel the block as it happens, make use of the energy and return the blow from another angle.

It is sometimes useful to slow Chi Sau right down and view individual moves, frame by frame, with one person attacking, the other defending. If an attack is successful or proves awkward to defend, you can rewind and try different counters until an appropriate one is found. The best option can then be sped up and drilled until it becomes natural. This is an effective way of understanding how simple footwork and hand shapes can work in many different ways. If you always practise at top speed you will never see all the options that are available, and will often use strength or pace to conceal elementary errors that could have been avoided in the first place. Your skill will be increased by patient critical analysis.

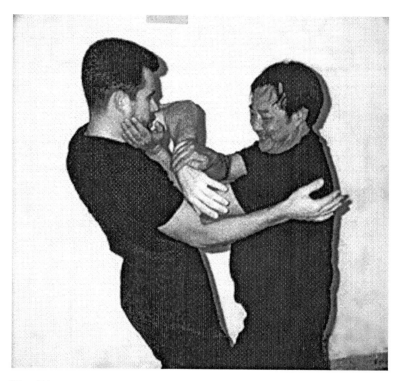

Pic. 76

Wong Shun Leung training Chi Sau with David Peterson

Overuse of strength and heavy handedness in Chi Sau will lead to stiff arms and over-committed attacks. These are easily dealt with because the intention is palpable; this creates an obvious choice of counter attack. Also, if your opponent has tense arms, this will enable you to gain control over their body; if you pull or push the arm, the body will move in an exploitable way. Any habits, quirks, or predictable behaviour in Chi Sau, can be seen as a weakness to be capitalised upon.

Chi Sau Roll, into Under-Laap

Often when people try to take you into a Laap Sau drill from Chi Sau, they will leave themselves open to being hit (off your Taan Sau arm) as soon as they attempt to grab your Fook Sau hand. Your Fook Sau hand may end up above, with your hitting hand underneath it. This works for two reasons: firstly, you are using Lat Sau Jik Chung so you are able to spring into the gap, and secondly, because your partner lifted their elbow in order to grab your hand. You can train this straight out of the roll and it is a good drill to train Lat Sau Jik Chung under the pressure of an attack. This is a good time to introduce and examine the Under-Laap (basically, the use of the Cham Kiu Fook Sau from beneath).

Pic. 77

A good method for training the Under-Laap is to start from the Chi Sau Roll After slightly crossing your partner's arms by bouncing the roll a little further than normal, thread your Fook Sau hand under your Bong and over their Fook arm (withdraw your Bong arm smartly at the same time). Your Under-Laap must travel through your partner's elbow, towards their opposite shoulder: this will control the body nicely. (Pic. 78) As this action is carried out, your footwork is following your leading hand diagonally through the stance. Your withdrawn hand now travels forward to attack the centre.

Pic. 78

To defend against this attack you will need to employ Lan Sau (Pic. 79), as in Cham Kiu form first section. This Lan Sau is ideal for dissipating pressure across your arms from the outside and towards the middle, whilst regaining a strong elbow position. As the Lan Sau is used you will need to track the moving target that is your partner's centre. You can also use Kwan Sau (Bong Sau and Taan Sau used in combination) to dissipate the Under-Laap.

Pic. 79

Chi Sau Roll, into Laap/Paak and Punch to Enter

From the Chi Sau Roll, cross your partner's arms and take them into go into Laap Sau. If they use Wu Sau to defend your attacking punch, catch the rear hand Wu Sau and Laap again to enter. Use Kwan Sau to dissolve this attack. An alternative to this drill is to use Paak Sau instead of Laap Sau after initially crossing the arms. This is actually more efficient, as the hand that is closest to the target is then hitting first.

Pic. 80a   Pic. 80b   Pic. 80c

Pic. 80d   Pic. 80e

Turbo Charge the Elbows

Start the Chi Sau Roll with both hands on inside or outside. The person using the outside Fook Sau presses in to give a resistance exercise to the person on the inside. This action also helps to force the Bong Sau and Taan Sau into the correct action. After a few rolls, the person feeding the pressure via Fook Sau grabs and pulls hard on the Taan Sau of the other person, attempting to drag them along. The inside roller now converts to Kwan Sau, steps in with the side that has been pulled as the lead leg and Bong Sau and charges down the instigator. This is technically termed stored elastic energy. Make sure you have plenty of space when training this drill!

Pic. 81

Tui Ma Retreat Drills from Chi Sau

From Chi Sau and using the entry step from single sticking hands, step in to your partner and press forward using Taan and Fook Sau. Do not reach in to push: use the stance and pressure from the legs. Taan Sau should press towards the shoulder area and Fook Sau should balance out the pressure on the forearm, making sure that it is central overall.

On receiving the pressure, allow your stance to be pressed back using Tui Ma. Maintain good structure, keeping pressure on the centre with Bong and Jam Sau. The instigator then repeats the push with Taan Sau and Fook Sau. Retreat a little further into the angle using the shuffle step, then use Paak and Fak Sau to attack back.

Pic. 82a

Pic. 82b

Pic. 82c

Pic. 82d

Alternatively use Under-Laap with the long step to the opposite side. This is made available because your Bong Sau is pressing and controlling the centre, preventing further attacks.

Pic. 83a   Pic. 83b

There are several variations on this drill that you can use in your training. From the same entry as for the above drill, retreat using Tui Ma but employ Lan Sau and Jam Sau to control the incoming attack off line. Then use Paak Sau and a strike to regain entry. This drill can then continue by adding double Huen Sau and re-pressing the centre after realigning the attack. Also try adding a shuffle step when going forwards to maintain momentum and pressure (and the same backwards to maintain position).

Jat Sau from Chi Sau

Press the Bong Sau into the central axis using the Fook Sau hand (this action is Jat Sau) and punch simultaneously. Cover the attack with Pau Bong Sau, Bong Sau or Kwan Sau. Then try utilising a suppressing Paak Sau to centre (over the incoming punch), followed with a long step to invite and enter on the next punch. Alternatively, you can follow the Paak Sau with Mun Sau to the opposite shoulder, controlling the enemy's lead arm at the elbow, with your elbow.

Pic. 84a

Pic. 84b

Pic. 84c

Pic. 84d

To make Chi Sau ideas and drills functional, we always need to practise scenarios and look at possible applications outside of the drill. This is elaborated later on in the sections on Fighting Practice and Fence and Reality drills.

Pic. 85a

Pic. 85b

Chi Geuk Drills

Chi Geuk (Sticking-legs Exercise) is normally practised separately from Chi Sau. Although it is possible to train both simultaneously, the range appropriate for legwork is somewhat closer, nearer grappling range, and tends to be more useful when normal positioning has broken down. Chi Geuk training is particularly handy if you wish to take control of an opponent, or take them to the ground, without punching or striking them.

Chi Geuk is also a good way to develop footwork that is resilient and responsive in the same way that the hands and arms should be. Start off facing your partner in forward stances, both with right legs forward and making contact from the knee to the foot. Hold on to your partner's shoulders; this is mainly to support each other should loss of balance occur and also to help isolate the legs and maintain squareness.

Pic. 86

Chi Geuk training

The instigator now attempts to sweep the lead leg of their partner away, using their own lead leg. As the leg is swept, allow the lower leg to rotate around the knee joint, in the same way that the elbow would normally work in Wing Chun. Whip your leg back around and under the instigators leg and controlling their knee with your own, press in and step forwards, under and through their stance. The end result of this manoeuvre should be that, as you move forwards, your thigh pushes the instigator's lead leg across and over their rear leg, collapsing and disrupting the stance.

Pic. 87a

Pic. 87b

Pic. 87c

Alternative options to this response are using a sidekick to the knee of the rear leg after being swept or using a front kick in the same situation. Strictly speaking, the sidekick is faster and more direct. However, if you use a front kick it is also possible to use the knee to control, as you would with the elbow, during your response. Be careful of your partner's knees during this drill, as they are very vulnerable and easily damaged when impacted from the side (which is of course the whole point).

Pic. 88a

Pic. 88b

Pic. 88c

It is then possible to practise a recovery from this technique after you have tried to sweep your partner. Start from the same position and attack, using the lead leg sweep. As your partner attempts to recover using any of the above concepts, plant your foot back down sharply using Huen Bo (Circle Step) from the Biu Ji Form whilst simultaneously turning your stance and body to face your partner. You should end up throwing them to the floor, which is why you are holding on to their shoulders to support them.

Pic. 89a

Pic. 89b

Impact Work

It is important to train to strike with impact. Punching against a wall bag, or with heavy focus mitts will do this. Performing palm strikes or punching against a wall bag filled with sand or beans, will help to develop penetrative striking power. It will also train the wrists, elbow position, strength, your use of stance and your whole body motion.

Pad work is very useful because you can train it from a stationary position, from a turn or pivot, whilst stepping forward to chase or whilst retreating. It is a skill in itself to feed good pad positions for your partner to strike at. You can also train to hit from a bad or compromised position, teaching yourself to attack as you recover; there are many demonstrations of this concept in the forms. Hitting a moving pad is excellent training for footwork, positioning and pre-Cham Kiu tracking and facing skills.

Practise hitting punch/wall bags with different types of blows, from unusual angles and from very close range. This will also teach you how to hit hard without over-committing your body weight. A heavy bag is also very good for linking the hands, waist and stance for powerful impact. Floor to ceiling balls are excellent for hand to eye co-ordination. These can be made simply by tying a tennis ball inside a pair of tights: tie the ball in the crotch then attach one foot to the ceiling and one to the floor.

The wooden dummy is a great training tool for correct striking and kicking. Kicks should be driven up from the floor, with pressure supplied by the rear leg. In this way any recoil from the dummy's support springs will be diverted back into your stance, and therefore the floor. If your body bounces back after hitting or kicking, you are not performing the action correctly. Be sure to kick with the heel, to avoid damaging your ankle and foot ligaments. You can train the same ideas in motion using a large, hand-held kick shield.

Strength and Conditioning

Strength and conditioning is an often-neglected aspect of Wing Chun, despite its pivotal role in any athletic endeavour. It should be obvious that to survive you must be both mentally and physically prepared for the rigours of combat. Proper strength and conditioning is therefore not an option, but a necessity.

The correct strength and conditioning required for Wing Chun is not just lifting weights, seeking a pump, going for the burn or performing a 5 mile run. It must be specific to the goal: that is, being as fast and as powerful as possible over a maximum of tens of seconds. Training should reflect this, with the development of such things as starting strength, explosive strength, anaerobic work capacity, speed and aggression. Training must either develop the required physical attributes in order to improve the application of technique (e.g. developing greater starting strength will allow faster and more powerful leg drive for punching off a fence position) and/or provide physical conditioning to help you to combat stress (e.g. repeated hill sprints with short rest periods between repetitions).

A special note on strength training is necessary, as it is often the most misunderstood aspect of strength and conditioning. A person should predominantly focus on heavy free weight compound exercises such as squats, dead lifts and Olympic lifts, with a safe and correct amount of weight for their current ability. Training should be limited to 2–3 times a week, because with the conditioning workouts and skill sessions, any more would negatively affect your ability to recuperate. You should use either a lower/upper body spilt or a total body split. Remember that as an athlete you need to be training movements, not muscle groups. The classic body part split routines that commonly feature in muscle magazines are not the best way to develop athletic ability.

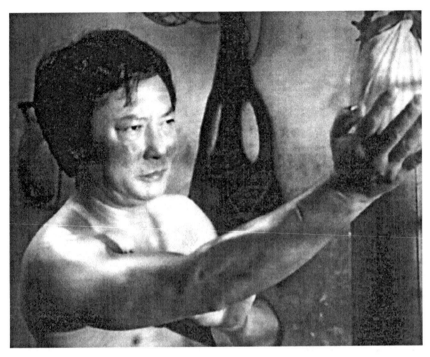

Pic. 90

Strength and conditioning are essential components for fighters

It is important to train safely, within your limits and, if possible, with another person to spot for you. Beware of taking advice from sports manual or personal trainers who are more geared towards bodybuilding and vanity. Instead seek out properly qualified power and Olympic-lifting coaches or strength and conditioning coaches who work with contact sports. Remember that no one source has all the answers: educate yourself to be able to separate the wheat from the chaff and understand that from one source you may need to heed some advice, whilst discarding others.

Fighting Practice

Whilst the technical training aspects of Wing Chun are all well and good, it is important to realise that all our skills may add up to nothing if we are not prepared to test ourselves and indulge in fighting itself.

What we have up to this point is a blueprint, a syllabus that will assist in preparation for fighting, but it's important to take the time to acknowledge that it is not actual fighting itself nor should it be viewed as such. Being a concept-based (as opposed to a technique-based) system, Wing Chun allows us a great deal of freedom in which to operate. However, without testing these concepts through fighting practice, the probability of failure is quite high.

Whilst I'm not advocating going out to your local pub and beating some poor fellow senseless, the aim of training is to prepare you both mentally and physically for a real life confrontation. The bottom line is, it doesn't matter how skilled you think you are, it's quite probable that in a real fight situation, you are going to get hurt. You must learn to accept this inevitability and develop the state of mind that enables you to fight on when injured and to inflict serious harm should it be necessary.

If we look back to some of the past seniors in Hong Kong, we can see that they didn't take things at face value; they actively went out and took part in Beimo (challenge matches), gaining valuable fighting experience and insights. My view is that if these guys went out and fought, tested what they were taught and made their Wing Chun functional, why shouldn't we? We are standing on the shoulders of giants, who helped forge and develop Wing Chun – is it there just to inherit as it is, or should we try and contribute something ourselves?

So, how do we go about getting fighting experience without it ending up a matter for the police? Quite simply by working with minimal protection, training with experienced fighters and working with people from other combative disciplines. Identify your weak points, then strengthen them. Get in there and fight. If you're looking at Chi Sau as fighting, then you're deluding yourself. Don't fall into the trap of speculating and hypothesising about what you think you would do with your untested skill: go out and accumulate some real experience of your own.

Pic. 91

Fighting practice

Fence and Reality Drills

This section looks more closely at how skills acquired through your Wing Chun training might apply to a real life situation. I am assuming that you are a law abiding citizen, not the aggressor, and that you have been forced into a situation where either you have to fight to defend yourself or you feel so threatened that striking first is your only reasonable option. Apart from being an essential training aid, scenario training is good fun and very cathartic when you put your heart into it. Train first against pads or heavy bags and then with a live partner; pushing, shouting and posturing should be added to build adrenaline and pressure testing into the equation.

Firstly, it is worth knowing that you are allowed to strike pre-emptively by law, if you feel threatened. Within the context of the martial arts, Geoff Thompson has defined the term 'fence', or guard, as a method of preventing an aggressor getting too close to you, whilst also subtly placing your own hands in an advantageous position from which you are free to defend or attack as necessary. You can also train for ways of gaining contact, in order to gain a strategic advantage during the pre-fight stages of combat.

In most threatening situations, my inclination is to begin with an attempt at pacifying the aggressor. I look them in the eyes and say that I do not want to fight them, but the message that I put across, both physically and psychologically, is that they will lose badly if they force me into a conflict. By telling them that I do not wish to fight, I am offering the aggressor a viable escape route and then reinforcing the attractiveness of this option by my physical presence and assertiveness. It is always safer not to fight at all if you can avoid it. You need to appear very confident and assertive to achieve this successfully, which is one reason why it is important to practise it through scenario training. It is very important to say the right things and act in an appropriate way when under the threat of violence. This normally involves attempting to de-escalate the situation verbally and calm the enemy down without appearing to be worried or intimidated by them.

Pic. 92

Aggressive behaviour

Asking a question, just prior to striking, is another excellent way of engaging the brain in order to cause a momentary distraction. The question can be anything from; 'Why are you picking on me?' To, 'What is the matter with you?' It does not even need to be relevant at all, but you need to practise a question followed immediately by striking a target, so that the question itself becomes a natural trigger. It is also good practice to think up a question that fits with your own character and is something that you will feel like saying when under pressure. We cannot, however, be sure that we will always have the luxury of contact or of any handy distraction, so we need to train for all eventualities.

In any case, the ideal is to line your enemy up so that you can attack them before they realise what you are doing. You don't want them to know that you are going to hit them, until after you have done. You then need to be relentless in your assault, not hesitating until the threat is eliminated. Initially your fence needs to be mobile and must not look as if you are going to fight (remember that you are trying to dissuade the person from fighting you). You should use your hands in a natural manner as if gesticulating, but you need to be acutely aware of where your (and your enemy's) attack lines lie.

Pleading Fence

If you have no contact to start with, hold you hands open and forward with the palms facing the enemy at about shoulder height, as if pleading. As the enemy attacks with a shove, grab or punch, manoeuvre your position into an attacking or retreating line and cover the incoming assault using your elbows as you attack back. This is not unlike using the Fook Sau concept to intercept punches described earlier.

Pic. 93a

Pic. 93b

First Contact

Use the hand behind the head pull from the first move of the dummy form, and pull the enemy onto your other elbow. To achieve the starting position, place your hand on their shoulder and turn your ear toward them, as if you cannot hear their threat clearly, then explode into action. This is especially effective in a noisy environment.

Pic. 94a

Pic. 94b

Pic. 94c

One Hand to Punch/Slap

From a single-handed guard push the enemy back or just check any forward movement. Using your free hand to gesticulate as you talk, subtly line them up for striking. Fractionally, after asking them a question, remove the pressure from your lead hand and strike them with your rear hand. A punch, palm strike or heavy slap will do the trick nicely here. All these strikes can easily be trained against pads or bags to develop power. Bear in mind that one of the effects of adrenaline is tunnel vision; accordingly it is good practice to train your pre-emptive strike from outside the line of peripheral vision. This will mean techniques like heavy palm strikes to the ears and jaw line, as opposed to straight-line punches.

Pic. 95a

Pic. 95b

Pic. 95c

Hands Pushed Off

It is worth remembering that if you do gain contact and put your hand on someone's chest, to prevent them pushing forward aggressively, they are very likely to shove your hand violently away again. This is another useful drill which can be trained by applying the various concepts of Single sticking hands to a static and then mobile fence/guard. It will also check that your shoulders remain relaxed whilst under stress.

Pic. 96a

Pic. 96b

Pic. 96c

Prevent a Shove

A powerful shove is often the prelude to further violence and blows, so train against this by using the retreat stepping drill with Jam Sau, Fook Sau, Paak Sau etc and follow up punches.

Pic. 97a

Pic. 97b

Pic. 97c

Accept a shove

It is a good idea to practise actually being pushed and then recovering your stance, as you may not have the time or the presence of mind to get to the Jam Sau and retreat step in time. Dai Jeung and Jeet Sau are possible techniques to utilise here, as are the pad work drills from deliberately poor positions.

Pic. 98a

Pic. 98b

Pic. 98c

Anti Fence Drills

It is also worth training with someone who uses a fence against you. It should be fairly apparent they are lining you up if you are switched on and aware of both their and your own positioning. If you have no contact, try to gain some, as this will work in your favour, allowing you to bring your pre-programmed Chi Sau skills into play. Alternatively, rather than relying on contact as an action trigger, you can use emotional sensitivity as a trigger. Other than this, you will need to be faster, more subtle or more assertive than the enemy. Think in terms of the recovery ideas that are given throughout the forms and practise striking pre-emptively and reactively from poor positions. You can also train getting into and out of bad positions in drills.

If someone has contact and a good line on you it is still possible to utilise ideas out of Cham Kiu and Siu Nim Tau for recovery. Bringing the elbows into play as in Fook Sau, Jam Sau or Bong Sau and even things like Jat Sau and Dai Jeung will work well when combined with sensitivity and footwork. Lan Sau works well if someone has grabbed you behind the neck, to pull you in or down.

Personal Development

Many attempts have been made to attach religious or philosophical meaning to the physical practice of kung fu. However, spirituality need not mean religion, anybody who is deeply involved in any art form will find some kind of spirituality through it. This is as true for martial arts as it is for music, painting or poetry. By immersing ourselves in our art we learn to express outwardly, something of our innermost self. Through this process of self-discovery, we can learn more about who we are and what we want; we hope that this is of benefit to ourselves and perhaps also a help to others.

Glossary

Baat Jaam Do ~ (Second Weapon Set Form) ~ Eight Slashing Knives Form or Butterfly Knives Form

Biu Ji ~ (Third Form) ~ Pointing Fingers Form

Biu Sau ~ Spearing-hand Attack

Bong Sau ~ Upper-arm Deflection

Cham Kiu ~ (Second Form) ~ Seeking The Bridge Form

Chau Kuen ~ Whipping Punch

Che Jeung ~ Descending-palm Strike

Chi Geuk ~ Sticking-legs Exercise

Chi Sau ~ Sticking-hands Exercise

Chi Sau Roll ~ (Also known as Luk Sau/Poon Sau Roll) ~ Rolling-hands Exercise

Chiu Ying ~ Square-on/Facing Concept

Daan Chi Sau ~ Single Sticking-hands Exercise

Daan Sau ~ Rebounding-hand Deflection

Dai Bong ~ Low Bong Sau

Dai Jeung ~ Lifting-palm Deflection

Dang Geuk ~ Ascending (Basic Heel) Kick

Dui Gok Ma ~ Side-facing Stance

Fak Sau ~ Whisking/Whipping-hand Attack

Fook Sau ~ Subduing-hand Deflection

Gaan Sau ~ Splitting-hand Deflection

Gwoh Sau ~ Free Attack Sticking-hands Exercise

Hoi Sung ~ taking advantage of an opponent's errors by following their centre of mass whenever they withdraw

Huen Bo ~ Circle Step

Huen Sau ~ Rolling-wrist Deflection

Jam (Jum) Sau ~ Sinking-arm Deflection

Jat (Jut) Sau ~ Jerking/Dragging-hand Deflection

Jeet Sau ~ Arm Wrenching

Jing Jeung ~ Standing-palm/Vertical-palm Strike

Juen Ma ~ Pivoting/Turning Footwork

Jui Ying ~ Chasing Concept

Kwan Sau ~ Bong Sau and Taan Sau used in combination

Laap Sau ~ Deflecting-hands Exercise

Lan Sau ~ Barrier-arm Deflection

Lat Sau Jik Chung ~ the concept of constant forward springy energy. For a full explanation, see 'Loi Lau Hoi Sung, Lat Sau Jik Chung' section

Loi Lau ~ Engaging with the Enemy

Luk Dim Boon Gwan ~ **(First Weapon Set Form)** ~ Six-and-a-half-point Long Pole Form, so called because the form only contains six and a half techniques

Muk Yan Jong ~ **(Fourth Form)** ~ Wooden Dummy Form

Mun Sau ~ Inquisitive Hand or Arm

Naat Sau ~ Pressing down Deflection

Paak Sau ~ Slapping-hand Deflection

Paau Bong Sau ~ Out of Contact or Casting Bong Sau often referred to as Emergency Bong Sau

Pei Jaang ~ Hacking Elbow

Saam Gok Bo ~ Advancing/Retreating Footwork

Saam Gok Ma ~ Advancing/Retreating Stance

Senk Sau ~ Scraping-hand Deflection

Seung Ma ~ Forward-attacking Footwork

Seung (Chi) Sau ~ Double Sticking-hands Exercise

Siu Nim Tau ~ **(First Form)** ~ Young Idea Form

Soh (Gum) Sau ~ Pressing-palm Deflection

Taan Sau ~ Spreading-hand Deflection

Tui Ma ~ Defensive (Sidestepping) Footwork or Push Step

Waang Geuk ~ Horizontal (Side) Kick

Waang Jeung ~ Lying-palm/Horizontal-palm Strike

Wu Sau ~ Guarding-hand Deflection

Yat Ji Kuen ~ Sun Character (Basic Vertical) Punch. 'Sun Character' refers to the Chinese character for the word sun, made up of three horizontal lines – very similar to the appearance of the fingers of the fist face on

Yi Bong Sau ~ In Contact or Shifting Bong Sau

Yi Ji Kim Yeung Ma ~ Character Two Goat Gripping Stance, so called because the legs form a shape that mimics the Chinese figure two: you stand as if restraining an animal between your legs

Yi Ying Sau ~ Shape-recovering Hand

Siu Nim Tau Form

Opening of Siu Nim Tau

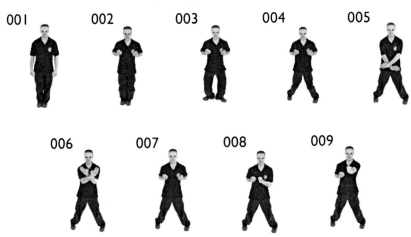

001 002 003 004 005

006 007 008 009

Huen Sau Stretch and Rear Elbow

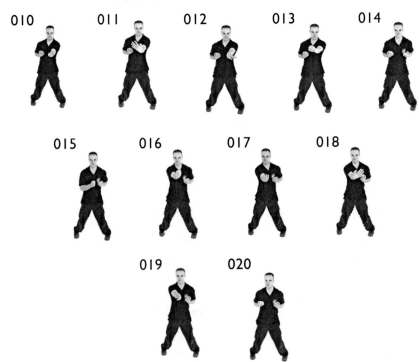

010 011 012 013 014

015 016 017 018

019 020

Section One

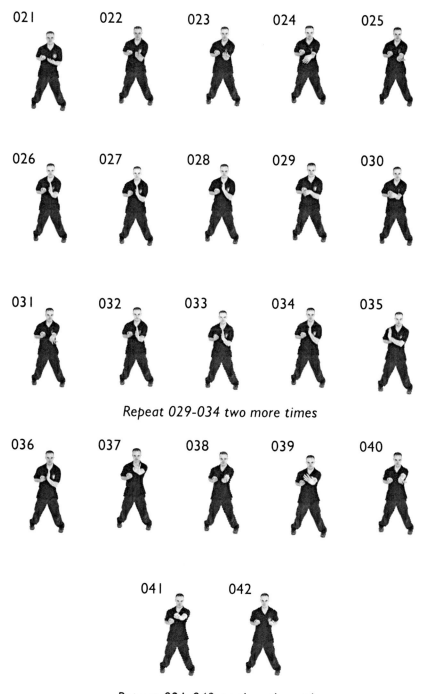

Repeat 029-034 two more times

Repeat 021-042 on the other side

Section Two

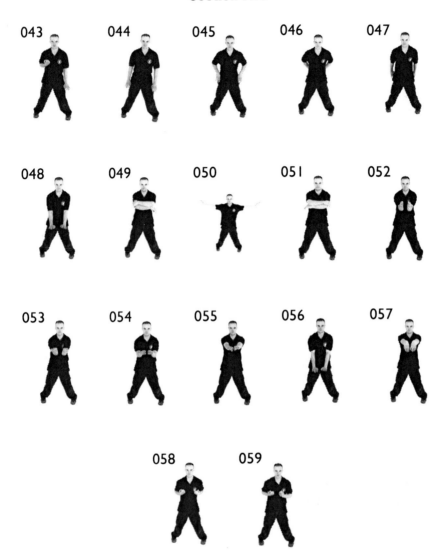

Section Three

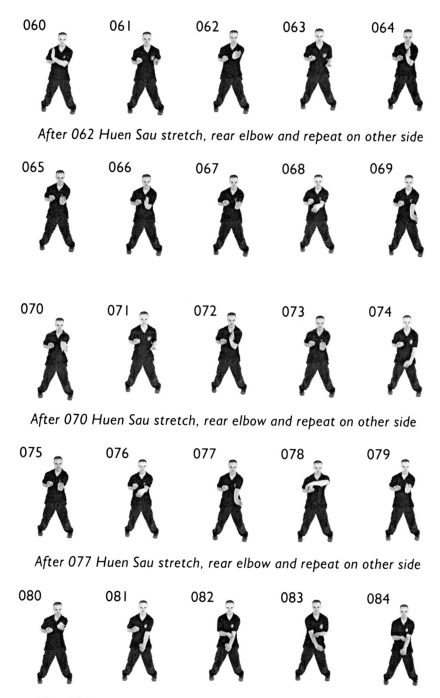

060 061 062 063 064

After 062 Huen Sau stretch, rear elbow and repeat on other side

065 066 067 068 069

070 071 072 073 074

After 070 Huen Sau stretch, rear elbow and repeat on other side

075 076 077 078 079

After 077 Huen Sau stretch, rear elbow and repeat on other side

080 081 082 083 084

After 080 Huen Sau stretch, rear elbow and repeat on other side

085   086   087   088   089

After 089 Huen Sau stretch, rear elbow and finish

Contact the Wing Chun Federation

The Wing Chun Federation was founded by Alan Gibson in 1990. The Federation's objective is to teach quality kung fu in a relaxed and accessible manner, where emphasis is placed on good technique and personal development. Wing Chun can be learnt simply by commitment and patience. A high level of proficiency can be obtained quickly and with relative ease.

Alan Gibson supplies an excellent range of DVDs, books and learning resources. He also runs regular seminars, where the student will learn the essentials of the Wing Chun system, as well as how to avoid dangerous or uncomfortable confrontations where possible.

To contact the Wing Chun Federation about lessons and seminars:

Alan Gibson

+44 (0)23 8057 2084

alan@wingchun.org.uk

www.wingchun.org.uk